MERE MISSIONS

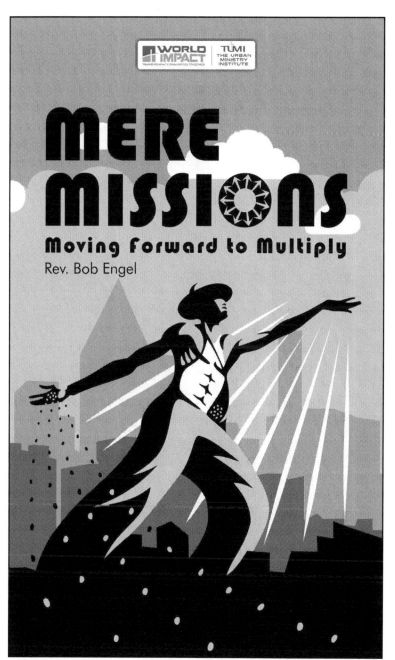

MERE MISSIONS

Moving Forward to Multiply

Rev. Bob Engel

TUMI Press
3701 East 13th Street North • Suite 100 • Wichita, Kansas 67208

To my wife, Susan, who is an amazing woman.

To the sung hero of missions, Paul the Apostle,
whom I can only dream of following as He has followed Christ.

To the unsung hero, Roland Allen. His four books have shaped me
as I have engaged in missions among the poor.

To the TUMI staff, with whom I co-labor in the Gospel.

To Rev. Dr. Don Davis, a mentor who has inspired me,
given me freedom to experiment,
caused me to laugh to the point of tears,
and has sharpened me in my calling.
He has been forged in iron that has sharpened me.

And to the Holy Spirit, the One who directs the expansion
and advancement of the Kingdom of God.

"... not of those who shrink back."
Hebrews 10.39b

TABLE OF CONTENTS

Appendix

FOREWORD

As one who counts it a great honor to be Bob's colleague and friend, I believe him to be one of the foremost global missions leaders in the Church of Jesus today. I am convinced that after carefully reading and engaging his reflections on missions in this book you will agree with my assessment. Why?

I could easily offer several tangible reasons to support this claim. First, Bob has served in various roles of missionary responsibility for nearly forty years, evangelizing and discipling in some of the most difficult communities of poverty in America. Also, he has planted churches in the city which grew to become healthy and effective outposts of kingdom display in tough, neglected neighborhoods. And, besides this, Bob has mentored, coached, trained, and released dozens of church planters and coaches called to plant healthy churches in communities of poverty, here in America and around the world. Truly, I cannot think of another single individual so well respected by the finest of the Lord's apostolic leaders around the world as Bob. His experience, humility, strategic passion, and burden for Christ and his Kingdom is compelling and evident, from the first moment you encounter him. In the language of the street, Bob is legit!

This small but remarkable text captures some of Bob's wealth of insights drawn from his own careful biblical reflection as well as his rich and relevant experience in winning people to Christ. This book contains the most basic principles and truths of mission, i.e., the critical foundation of thinking why we should do Gospel missions in the world today. When many leaders and denominations are advocating for the end of classic Gospel mission (i.e., evangelism, discipleship, and church-planting), Bob advocates for a return to "mere missions," a play on C. S. Lewis's classic text, *Mere Christianity*.

In the same spirit as Lewis's key summary work, Bob's *Mere Missions* lays out what must be considered as a crash course in biblical missions approaches and truths, making it an essential "Missions 101" text. Not just for those called to church planting and evangelism, this book should be widely read and studied by anyone interested in getting a firm grasp on the perspective, vision, and strategies to do effective twenty-first century cross-cultural Gospel missions work. Starting from the assumption that biblical missions is still both valid and necessary in today's world, he lays out an effective strategy that takes the apostolic witness and historical experience about the proclamation of Christ seriously. It is written with the clarity of a skilled practitioner and with the heart of an apostolically gifted leader with much to teach on how to represent Christ in unreached neighborhoods of poverty.

Mere Missions deserves a slow, prayerful, and thoughtful read. It highlights the urgency for the Gospel in our ever-changing society and world, and bluntly identifies the vast numbers of people who have yet to hear of God's love in Christ. He pulls no punches. For Bob, the stakes could not be higher, and this present time could not be more critical. Those of us who love the Gospel of Jesus Christ must redouble our efforts immediately to rediscover the nature of the missionary call and enterprise, and do all that we can to make our contribution count, while time remains. This is Bob's heart-plea for us to join the fight! May he prove successful, challenging us rediscovering what *Mere Missions* is, that we may better learn to tell the story of life and hope in Christ to a dying and lost world.

Don L. Davis
June 15, 2022

PREFACE

After receiving all authority in heaven and on earth, Jesus said to His disciples, "Therefore, go and make disciples of all nations, baptizing them in the name of the Father and of the Son and of the Holy Spirit, and teaching them to obey everything I have commanded you. And surely, I am with you always, to the very end of the age" (Matt. 28.19-20). The Kingdom of God has entered the world and the King of this Kingdom gave a mission charge to get up, get out and to "move forward and multiply." This movement cannot help but move forward for it is directly related to the character, being, and thought of God Almighty. "For God so loved the world (the character of God – love, mercy, compassion), that he gave his only Son (the being of God – missions, sending, initiating), that whoever believes in him should not perish but have eternal life. For God did not send his Son into the world to condemn the world, but in order that the world might be saved (the thought of God – salvation, hope, rescue) through him" (John 3.16-17). This same character, being and thought of God is now within us, His Church. This is the deepest motive for missions. It is in our spiritual DNA.

Since that charge the Kingdom has been advancing and expanding, like a mustard seed (Matt. 13.31-32), in a world bound and enslaved in a Kingdom of Darkness ruled by a real spiritual demonic tyrant. The Church, though flawed and imperfect, has been faithful in the mission. The proof? You and me. We are disciples of the Nazarene because someone proclaimed the Gospel of Jesus to us and the Lord of the Harvest rescued us in our cry, "have mercy on me" (Luke 18.38). This line of "beautiful feet" (Rom. 10.15) who brought us good news is traced back to the obedience of the early Church who faithfully witnessed to the Lordship of Jesus. I love the Great Commission. I'm indebted to Christ the Victor who commissioned His Apostles to move forward and multiply so that one day I could respond to the Good News of, "the righteousness of God through faith in Jesus Christ for all who believe" (Rom. 3.21). And now, it has been my turn, it is our turn, to keep moving forward in missions in order to multiply.

I resonate with the writer of Ecclesiastes when he cast this bit of wisdom, "There's no end to the publishing of books, and constant study wears you out so you're no good for anything else" (Eccles. 12.12). So why write a book? Each year approximately 1,000,000 books are written. What is book 1,000,001 going to contribute to the complexities of missions in the post-modern twenty-first century? I defer to the insightful words of A. W. Tozer who wrote, "The only book that should ever be written is one that flows up from the heart, forced out by the inward pressure." For four decades of urban ministry among the poor, the principles of missions that I have learned, in many cases the hard way, have trickled out at various times and opportunities. I write this booklet to open the faucet and relieve the inward pressure flowing up from my heart for missions and my love for the Lord Jesus. That alone would suffice in relieving the pressure within my heart but if there is even one who is inspired and applies the mission nuggets that I share, then that would be an added blessing.

I originally had a different title to this book but made a change after re-reading C. S. Lewis's classic book, *Mere Christianity*. In his preface, Lewis defines 'mere' Christianity as consisting of those beliefs that have been "common to all Christians at all times." Adopting that vein of thought, *Mere Missions: Moving Forward to Multiply* consists of those principles that are common, prevalent, to missions at all times. C. S. Lewis probably had his detractors to *Mere Christianity*. I do not put myself on the level of C. S. Lewis so I'm sure there will be those who will disparage, and challenge *Mere Missions*. I'm okay with that. I welcome conversation, not condemnation. I aptly cling to the words of David, "Search me, O God, and know my heart! Try me and know my thoughts! And see if there be any grievous way in me and lead me in the way everlasting!" (Ps. 139.23-24).

C. S. Lewis, in dealing with the subject matter of *Mere Christianity*, said in his preface, "I am only a layman, and at this point we are getting into deep water. I can only tell you, for what it is worth, how I, personally, look at the matter." I, too, am only a layman. I am not a missiologist. I have no higher education degrees. Like Lewis, I can only tell, you, for what it is worth, how I, personally, look at the matter of missions and the Church. As J. Herbert Kane said, "When the Church has been true to her own genius, she has always been a witnessing community. When she has lost her missionary vision, she has turned inward and gone into decline. But whenever she has experienced revival, she has always resumed her essential task – world missions."

There is nothing new under the sun (Eccles. 1.9). Eric Hoffer in his book, *The True Believer: Thoughts on the Nature of Mass Movements*, said it like this, "The great Christian revolutions come not by the discovery of something that was not known before. They happen when someone takes radically something that was already there." This book is a reminder, a renewal back to old foundations that are timeless and cross into all cultures. This book on missions is not a fire hydrant in which you will be overwhelmed by its volume and force. It is a faucet. My prayer is that as you turn on the faucet you might be able to fill your cup to drink and be refreshed and inspired to not shrink back and continue to keep moving forward for the expansion and advancement of God's Kingdom, by the grace of God and in the power of his Holy Spirit.

Bob Engel

June 2022

INTRODUCTION

A church which is not deeply penetrated by the faith that the crucial center of all human history is what God has done, in and through Christ, will hardly undertake a sustained missionary effort, and its witness will never have the toughness and resiliency, the patience and the endurance without which missions cannot accomplish their task.

~ G. W. Peters, *A Theology of Missions*

For I see violence and strife in the city. Day and night they prowl about on its walls; malice and abuse are within it. Destructive forces are at work in the city; threats and lies never leave its streets.

~ Psalm 55.9-10

I understand these verses. I have seen the violence and strife in the city both day and night take place. Gang members shooting at each other during a Bible Club taking place on my front lawn; Being threatened when attending a black Muslim meeting at my local community center; hearing the gun shots and arriving first to see the lifeless body of a young pregnant girl slumped in the front seat of her car. Or what would cause a young teen to shave half his eyebrow, tattoo "666" in that spot, give himself the street name "Satan", and attempt to kill his grandma? Or ministering to a young girl, whose pimp yanked the earrings out of her lobes, beat her, threw her into cactus patch, and left her for dead? Nothing has changed since King David wrote this about his beloved city of Jerusalem over four thousand years ago. The destructive forces at work in the world are real, relentless, reckless and show no partiality to age, gender, class or ethnicity.

In addition, these forces war against the Kingdom of God, and all of humanity is born into the middle of these two kingdoms that are in conflict. It was C. S. Lewis who wrote, "Enemy-occupied territory – that is what this world is. Christianity is the story of how the rightful king has landed, you might say landed in disguise, and is calling us to take part in a great campaign of sabotage." This book is about the "great campaign of sabotage" that we have been called, actually mandated, to participate in. In a sense, we become Kingdom Saboteurs in "enemy-occupied-territory." Or as the title of my book states it, "*Mere Missions: Moving Forward to Multiply.*"

For the Church to best move forward in missions its critical to have a clear understanding of the three important mandates God has communicated in Scripture and to whom they are communicated to. *The first mandate was given to everyone as a member of the human race.* It is philanthropic and humanitarian service rendered by people to people on the human level. We were given the responsibility and joy to develop a wholesome culture in which to live and thrive, that is built upon fellowship with our Creator, to love others as we love ourselves, and to upkeep our world. This mandate is given to us under the banner of being a member of humanity and not the banner of being a member of the Church.

When sin entered our world, it made the responsibility an impossibility. All the systems that make up a healthy culture –

religion, family, commerce, politics, law, education, habitat, health, environment – have now been corrupted by the cancerous effects of sinful humanity. If left unchecked, humanity would annihilate each other, completely strip, and pollute all that is beautiful on this planet and seek their own worship and fame rather than their Creator. God, whose love (agape) knows no bounds, would not let this go unchecked. In Christ Jesus, He brought reconciliation and restoration, and began to reverse the effects of sin. A foretaste of the Kingdom of God was initiated with its completion taking place with the return of the Son of God. It is then that there will be unhindered fellowship and worship with our God; genuine love between all nations, tribes and people; and a new heaven and earth in which to dwell (Rev. 21.1). Until this return of the King, God has not absolved humanity from this mandate, and we continue to strive towards a wholesome world in which to live and survive.

Mandate number two is given by the Lord Jesus to His disciples. Its focus is directed towards those inside the Kingdom Society, His sisters and brothers, and not to all of humanity. It's the new commandment from the Lord when He said, "A new commandment I give to you, that you love one another: just as I have loved you, you also are to love one another" (John 15.12). When we demonstrate this love in action within the Kingdom Society through addressing racism (neither Jew nor Gentile) sexism (male nor female), classism (rich nor poor), Jesus said the world would know we are His followers (Acts 2.42-47; Acts 6; Gal. 2.11-14; 1 John 3.23). If we are to be a witness to the unbelieving lost in the world, we must begin with our love for one another. If an "outsider" is looking "inside" the Church and sees racism, sexism, classism, and division rather than unity (John 17.21-23), or minimally, the intentional effort of those claiming to be a disciple of Jesus working together to genuinely address these issues, then why would the "outsider" want to come "inside?" They already see and experience this in the world that is all around them. We must put aside childish ways (1 Cor. 13.11) and be aggressive and intentional in loving one another. We are brothers and sisters (Eph. 1.5) from the same household of faith (Gal. 6.10); a chosen race, a royal priesthood, a holy nation (1 Pet. 2.9).

The third mandate from the Lord Jesus is also given to His followers as members of the Kingdom Society. Its focus is towards those outside the Church to all who are spiritually dead (Eph. 2.1) and at enmity with God (Rom. 8.7; James 4.4). It is a mandate to "Go therefore and make disciples of all nations, baptizing them in the name of the Father and of the Son and of the Holy Spirit, teaching them to observe all that I have commanded you. And behold, I am with you always, to the end of the age." We have been entrusted with a message that liberates (Gal. 5.1), reconciles (2 Cor. 5.18), and restores (1 Pet. 2.24) the fellowship with God for all those who by faith confess Jesus as Lord and believe in their hearts that He is alive (Rom. 10.9). This mandate does not negate, supersede, duplicate, or absorb the first or second mandate. It stands on its own. It is carried forward by evangelism leading to discipleship and church planting.

This mandate was not given to humanity but was given to all those who claim Jesus Christ as Lord and is considered missions in the strict biblical sense of "the sending forth of authorized persons to unchurched communities to proclaim the Gospel in order to win converts to Jesus Christ, make disciples from the converts, and gather together the disciples to form functioning, multiplying local churches that bear the fruit of the Kingdom of God in that community" (Acts 13.1-3; Acts 26.18; Eph. 4.11 [some are apostolic in gift and calling]; Jon. 3; Mark 16.15; Matt. 28.19-20; Luke 24.47; John 20.22-23). All God's children are to honor Christ the Lord in our hearts as holy, always being prepared to make a defense to anyone who asks us for a reason for the hope that is in us yet doing it with gentleness and respect (1 Pet. 3.15). This is different in that certain individuals within the

Kingdom Society are authorized and sent (Acts 3.1-3) with the task to win converts to Jesus through Gospel proclamation leading to the establishing of functioning, multiplying communities of the Kingdom who will, as disciples of the Lord Jesus, be obedient to the second and third mandates. I will talk more about these in the chapter on the Gospel.

Keeping the three mandates distinguished will keep the Church clear and, give freedom and wisdom to maximize the stewardship of her time talent, and treasure. It is not the mission of the church to aim at the total reorganization of the whole social value and fabric. That is the mission of humanity, and as I already mentioned, we are failing and heading for destruction.

What we can be assured of, however, is that the early Christian church were not merely interested in the disembodied souls of the lost. The Nazarene argued that we would be judged in how we responded to the hungry, thirsty, naked, stranger, the sick, and the prisoner. Wherever the Gospel was accepted, believers demonstrated the power and grace of Christ in tangible deeds of love, justice, and hospitality. Believers started the first hostels, some of the first hospitals for the poor, and performed works of generosity and mercy for the outcast and the broken. Even in the writings of Christianity's earliest detractors Christians are described as the defenders of the image of God in every person in society. They even cared for slaves, children, and women! Literally, to be a believer was to shine a light that revealed the justice, freedom, and wholeness of the Kingdom before unbelieving eyes and hearts. Believers in their acts of charity and grace proved themselves true to Christ's injunction: "Your light must shine before people in such a way that they may see your good works, and glorify your Father who is in heaven" (Matt. 5.16, ESV).

So, the pathway of the Gospel for world transformation appeared, at first glance, to take a less-than-direct approach toward societal change. The apostles did not aim directly at such an end. Neither did Jesus. They did not become involved in processions against Roman police brutality, slavery, social or economic injustices, marches for civil rights, higher wages, or better education. Jesus authorized no one to do such. He authorized and mandated His disciples to love each other and to go proclaim Good News, make disciples, leading to new churches being established for the glory of God and the expansion of His Kingdom. In fact, some might even argue, that we see the opposite in the Lord Jesus.

Tucked away in the Gospel of Luke is the following story of an encounter Jesus had that reveals the reality of eternity that Jesus was so aware of. "There were some present at that very time who told him about the Galileans whose blood Pilate had mingled with their sacrifices. And he answered them, "Do you think that these Galileans were worse sinners than all the other Galileans, because they suffered in this way? No, I tell you; but unless you repent, you will all likewise perish" (Luke 13.1-3). Jesus was a Galilean Jew. Though of mutual descent, religion, and ethnicity, they were culturally different than Judean Jews. Galileans came to Jesus, one of their own, expecting compassion and outrage mingled together. I'm sure they thought Galilean lives would matter to Jesus given not only His cultural connection but also because of the brutality and injustice of the Roman police force. This most certainly demands a response, an outcry, a protest from Jesus. Added to that was the disrespect to their religion, their God, His God, and Father. It was a social and religious injustice of epic proportion. Surely Jesus would do something.

As the Son of Man, he didn't do anything. There was no protest or the formation of an organization to address this atrocity. As the Son of God though, He had a response. Pointing them to eternal matters, He said, "Unless you repent, you will all likewise perish." It can seem to the "temporal eye" that Jesus is cold, un-caring, unsympathetic. Where is His humanity? Where is His pastoral heart in such a tragedy as this? Or what about the justice that is to, "roll down as waters, and righteousness as a mighty stream" (Amos 5.4). Yet the "eternal eye" of the Son of God, allowed Him to communicate the most caring, sympathetic, pastoral and just of all responses to be given to man(kind), "Unless you repent, you will all likewise perish." The Greek word used for perish is, permanent (absolute) destruction, i.e. to cancel out (remove); "to die, with the implication of ruin and destruction"; cause to be lost (utterly perish) by experiencing a miserable end. What could be more caring, sympathetic, pastoral, and just than this? "For what does it profit a man to gain the whole world [social justice] and forfeit his soul? For what can a man give in return for his soul?" (Mark 8.36-37).

Mere Missions is ultimately about the salvation of human beings, the salvation of their "souls." The Lord has bound (Matt. 12.29), disarmed (Col. 2.15) and inflicted a wound into our spiritual enemy that now allows souls to be set free (Luke 4.18) from the bondage and tyranny that all have been born into. Humanity is liberated from the chains of sin and death that Satan kept us in bondage to and, he himself, is now bound as a captive. The Gospel is the power that sets souls free when received in obedient faith. It was for freedom that Christ Jesus set us free (Gal. 5.1). This freedom, however, results in life-transforming good deeds done to our friends, families, and neighbors. These works of kindness, justice, and righteousness give full demonstration of the grace that has touched our souls and given birth to these works we do: "For we are His workmanship, created in Christ Jesus for good works, which God prepared beforehand so that we would walk in them" (Eph. 2.10). The soul that claims to be saved should walk in the works that God has prepared for her or him to do; faith without works, in every case, is really dead (James 2.14-26).

So, we see the challenge to be clear. The Holy Spirit directs the church to souls (with the biblical allusion to the eternal part of human life) that are being saved. The Church receives these souls into a new family where racism, sexism, classism, and division are addressed so that the world would see our love for each other and our unity. The Kingdom, God's rule and reign, His domain, is directed towards the eternal destiny of souls. Missions is our part in God's mandate to participate with Him to "search and rescue" souls.

While this language of "souls" may at first glance seem either naïve or even archaic, I believe that it is the language of Scripture. Such language, however, does not discount the reality of human life as a body-soul-spirit reality. When God redeems a soul, the body becomes a temple of the Holy Spirit (1 Cor. 6.19-20), and the spirit is sealed with the very Spirit of God (Eph. 1.13). My emphasis on souls is not a denial of our human existence; it is to say that the eternal destiny of every person is at stake in the Gospel. To deny this is unbiblical, and to describe human life as only a "soul affair" is unbiblical as well. (The early Gnostics asserted that the soul alone was important, and that the body was unimportant and irrelevant. Such teaching was rejected as unchristian as early as the first century).

As I have participated with the God of missions, I have found that the best rule of engagement is simplicity. I am not saying simplistic. There is a difference. Simplicity means to take complex issues, like the theology of missions, and make them easy to understand or do. Simplistic, on the other hand, is treating complex issues and problems as if they were much simpler than they really are. A simplistic approach to missions may well create and add to the complexity creating deeper and more complicated problems. Understanding the difference has impacted the way I have approached ministry and missions among the poor and will be reflected in this book. Each chapter has the following same flow, creating a simple grasp on the focus being covered:

Contact: Situation Awareness

I will share a story, mostly from my own journey in missions, giving my awareness of the situation. The story will help unfold the missions plank (a fundamental and foundational point) we will focus on in the chapter.

Content 1: Missions Plank

In this section I will share my biblical viewpoint and personal insights to add comprehension on one of the five planks of missions (Jesus Is Lord. The Gospel. The Church. The Holy Spirit. The Kingdom). These five planks make up an *Apostolic Missions Platform*.

Content 2: "E" of an Apostolic Missions Platform

Governments are comprised of political parties and what distinguishes the different party members is their "party platform", that is, their set of principles and actions designed to address their mission. As I have engaged in mission, I have concluded that God's Kingdom Government platform for His members (disciples), can be summed up with six actions. These six actions are represented by an "E." One "E" for each of our five planks of an *Apostolic Missions Platform*. These five outward actions are simple yet will demand an intentional decision flowing out of a comprehensive understanding of the Missions Plank. The sixth "E" is an internal action rooted in the exhortation and life of the Lord Jesus and of His Apostles therefore making our missions platform an apostolic platform. By *apostolic* I simply mean that each action was reflected in the apostles who were appointed and authorized and sent out for missions.

Connection: Rules of Engagement (ROE)

In this last section of the chapter, I will share ROEs to assist in an *Apostolic Missions Platform Response*. These are practical engagements designed to keep the Church and the church planter focused on moving forward in Apostolic missions. I include the Church in the ROEs because there is no church planter if there is no Church, for the Church is the sending authority. The section will end with a *Connection Story* of a saint, unknown to the Church yet known by me and to our God. The story might not be dynamic in and of itself, but it was dynamically used in my life. These unknown saints, living in some of the poorest most violent communities around the world, were used by the Holy Spirit to conform me more into the image of Jesus (Rom. 8.29) and to form the *Apostolic Missions Platform* that now drives my calling in mission. They would not want their story to be long for they are the meek and humble friends I have known who are used of God to advance His Kingdom as we both journey towards our eternal home.

The Kingdom of God, His rule and reign, has, is and will continue to always move forward. It is expanding and advancing to the end that the earth be filled with the knowledge and glory of the Lord as the waters cover the sea (Hab. 2.14). Nothing or no one can hinder, stop or destroy this movement. Not even the gates of hell itself (Matt. 16.18). Until then, as people of this Kingdom we must keep moving forward. There is no room for cowards in the Kingdom by shrinking back (Rev. 21.8; Heb. 10.35-39). May you find wise guidance to help you in the spiritual war we find ourselves in and cannot escape (Prov. 24.6).

Chapter 1

JESUS IS LORD: Endearment

Key Old Testament Verse

"Enoch walked with God . . ."

~ Genesis 5.24a

Key New Testament Verse

"I am the true vine, and my Father is the vinedresser. Every branch in me that does not bear fruit he takes away, and every branch that does bear fruit he prunes, that it may bear more fruit. Already you are clean because of the word that I have spoken to you. Abide in me, and I in you. As the branch cannot bear fruit by itself, unless it abides in the vine, neither can you, unless you abide in me. I am the vine; you are the branches. Whoever abides in me and I in him, he it is that bears much fruit, for apart from me you can do nothing. If anyone does not abide in me he is thrown away like a branch and withers; and the branches are gathered, thrown into the fire, and burned. If you abide in me, and my words abide in you, ask whatever you wish, and it will be done for you. By this my Father is glorified, that you bear much fruit and so prove to be my disciples. As the Father has loved me, so have I loved you. Abide in my love. If you keep my commandments, you will abide in my love, just as I have kept my Father's commandments and abide in his love. These things I have spoken to you, that my joy may be in you, and that your joy may be full.

~ John 15.1-11

Contact: Situation Awareness

"I can't wait till Jesus takes me up in the air like that." Those words sealed the direction of my life journey and it started in the spring of 1982. I was in my Senior year at Taylor University, majoring in Christian Education. January, known as J-Term, was always quiet and peaceful on campus. Many students went to other schools or took trips during this light academic load month. Usually, they went somewhere where it was warm and sunny to escape the frigid cold and cornfields of Indiana. Like the three previous years I chose to go back to Taylor. It's not that I necessarily liked the cold but the quiet and slowness of campus life during this time was perfect to reflect on my future plans upon graduation. I was a regular visitor to the small prayer chapel, across from my dorm, where I could pray and journal. As I reflected on my life experiences at Taylor, the Spirit of the Lord made four truths very clear to me: 1) God's heart for the poor and oppressed (Jon. 4.11); 2) disciples are to be salt and light in a decaying and dark world (Matt. 5.13-16); 3) the Lords deep love for His Bride, the Church (Rev. 19.6-8); and 4) God's missions mandate to go and make disciples (Matt. 28.18-20; 2 Tim. 2.2). There it was. Four years wrapped up into four foundational principles. So, what next? Where do I go? "Lord, show me clearly what it is you want from me."

Around this time of searching and praying I was reading the book *The Making of a Disciple* by Dr. Keith Phillips. Along with a female counterpart, we were leading a campus wide discipleship program and I was always looking for some further insights. I was so challenged by the book that I had to know more about the author. I looked on the jacket cover and read about World Impact, "a nationwide, interdenominational discipling ministry that seeks to bring God's love to the ghettos of America." There it was. As clear as clear could be. The Holy Spirit revealed the next phase of my journey as a young twenty-one-year-old disciple of Jesus. "The ghettos of America!" But wait! I didn't know much about the ghetto (old school word meaning 'isolation') but what I did know didn't seem like the right fit.

"Lord are you sure about this?" "Did I hear your still small voice correctly?" "I'm 5'9 . . . and-a-half!" "I weigh 118 pounds!" My strongest drug was orange flavored children's aspirin. My mom was the "drug dealer" in our home and she only dispensed of the powerful orange drug sparingly. My strongest drink was Dr. Pepper "on the rocks." I don't play basketball (my vertical was about two inches). The only incarceration experience I had was being confined to my room when I got into trouble as a child. There must be a mistake. But the Lord doesn't make mistakes or accept excuses. It is not what I think, but what He says. Jesus is Lord and all He requires is that I trust Him (Prov. 3.5-6). His ways are not my ways, and neither are His thoughts my thoughts (Isa. 55.8). He expects obedience. As Dietrich Bonhoeffer said, "The one who believes, obeys, and the one who obeys, believes" (*The Cost of Discipleship*). My only response must be, "Yes Lord!"

Upon graduation, my roommate, Steve Long, and I rode bicycles from Upland, Indiana, to Lake Tahoe (2,121 miles), which is along the state line of California and Nevada. We spent the summer evangelizing with CRU. After an incredible summer I made my way to Los Angeles and through some remarkable circumstances found my way to World Impact for a three-day interview and ministry exposure. The first day, I was with a World Impact urban missionary who was making a home visit in Imperial Courts Housing Projects in South Central, home of the PJ Watts Crips. To say the least, I was completely out of my comfort zone.

There were gang members hanging out, drug deals going down, prostitutes on the corner. I had "crossed-over" into a world that was completely different from the world I grew up in. In the midst of my culture shock, a six-year-old African American boy in cut off shorts, no shirt, no shoes, and nappy hair, came running across a trash studded dirt field and jumped into my arms with the biggest grin imaginable. I began to toss him in the air, laughing, and feeling a bit more comfortable. At one point, this little boy, whose name I don't remember, looked into my eyes and said, "I can't wait till Jesus takes me up in the air like that." A new awakening seized me. Someone entered his "world" of gangs, drugs, violence and, what seemed to be hopelessness, and spoke a simple eternal truth that Jesus is Lord and His Kingdom is real and beyond this world. Anyone can enter the narrow gate by faith. This little boy believed and entered. He saw the Kingdom of God. The same Lord who called me to communities of poverty to represent Him and His Kingdom was the same Lord who called this little boy to what was, "really real." It was the "really real" that the Apostle Paul reminded the Corinthian believers when he wrote, "For this light momentary affliction is preparing for us an eternal weight of glory beyond all comparison, as we look not to the things that are seen but to the things that are unseen. For the things that are seen are transient, but the things that are unseen are eternal" (2 Cor. 4.17-18).

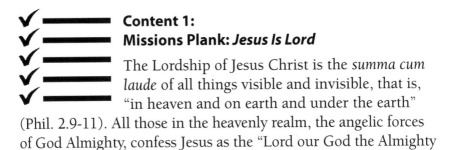

Content 1:
Missions Plank: *Jesus Is Lord*

The Lordship of Jesus Christ is the *summa cum laude* of all things visible and invisible, that is, "in heaven and on earth and under the earth" (Phil. 2.9-11). All those in the heavenly realm, the angelic forces of God Almighty, confess Jesus as the "Lord our God the Almighty who reigns" (Rev. 19.6). All those under the earth, the demonic cosmic forces and their rulers and authorities, all confess and shriek with terror at the Lordship and authority of Jesus (Matt. 8.28-34). It is strange that though the spiritual beings in the heavenly world and the underworld have no doubts as to the Lordship of Jesus, there are those on the earth who question, doubt, and even fight against it. King David captured it well in Psalm 2.1-4, "Why do the nations rage and the peoples plot in vain? The kings of the earth set themselves, and the rulers take counsel together, against the Lord and against his Anointed, saying, 'Let us burst their bonds apart and cast away their cords from us.' He who sits in the heavens laughs; the Lord holds them in derision." Jesus is the Lord, "and the ruler of kings on earth" (Rev. 1.5).

The declaration that Jesus is Lord goes deep into the sacred roots of the Church's Great Tradition – "those doctrines, practices, and structures employed by the ancient Church as it sought to give expression to the truth concerning Jesus Christ" (*Sacred Roots: A Primer on Retrieving the Great Tradition, Dr. Don. L. Davis*). Some say that these three words, *Jesus is Lord*, sum up the Christian faith.

The Apostles' first-hand experience with Jesus of Nazareth as written in our Bible today, gives witness to over 650 times to the truth that Jesus is Lord. This is the heart of apostolic preaching and proclamation, "For what we proclaim is not ourselves, but Jesus Christ as Lord, with ourselves as your servants for Jesus's sake" (2 Cor. 4.5). On the Day of Pentecost when the Church was birthed by the Holy Spirit, Peter stood before the nations that had gathered in Jerusalem and confessed "Let all the house of Israel therefore know for certain that God has made him both Lord and Christ, this Jesus whom you crucified" (Acts 2.36). The Apostle Peter was not preaching a wishful thought, possibility or probability. It was a certainty.

The Ecumenical Councils, as written in all four of the major Creeds when the church was one and undivided, confess that Jesus is Lord:

- Apostles Creed (120-250 A.D.) – "I believe in Jesus Christ, his only Son, our Lord"

- Nicene Creed (325 A.D.) – "We believe in one Lord Jesus Christ . . ."

- Chalcedonian Creed (451 A.D.) – "One and the same Christ, Son, Lord, Only-begotten . . ."

- Athanasian Creed (500 A.D.) – "So likewise . . . the Son Lord"

The Ancient Rule of Faith, "that which has always been believed, everywhere, and by all," has faithfully affirmed that Jesus is Lord when heresy has attempted to shake and break this foundational confession of the Church. No matter how far back you go (always); what continent, country or island (everywhere); or what tribe, language or people (by all), the Church confesses that Jesus is Lord.

What God Himself declares about Himself becomes the final matter whether one believes it or not for, "God is not a man, that he should lie; neither the son of man, that he should repent: hath he said, and shall he not do it? or hath he spoken, and shall he not make it good?" (Num. 23.19). The Trinity has "made it good" by declaring Jesus is Lord:

- God the Father Almighty, "has highly exalted him [Jesus] and bestowed on him the name that is above every name, so that at the name of Jesus every knee should bow, in heaven and on earth and under the earth, and every tongue confess that Jesus Christ is Lord, to the glory of God the Father" (Phil. 2.8-11).

- God the Son declared to Pilate, "My kingdom is not of this world. If my kingdom were of this world, my servants would have been fighting, that I might not be delivered over to the Jews. But my kingdom is not from the world... You say that I am a king. For this purpose, I was born and for this purpose I have come into the world—to bear witness to the truth. Everyone who is of the truth listens to my voice" (John 18.36-37)

- God the Holy Spirit, "Therefore I want you to understand that no one speaking in the Spirit of God ever says, 'Jesus is accursed!' and no one can say 'Jesus is Lord' except in the Holy Spirit knowledge that Jesus is Lord" (1 Cor. 12.3).

The declaration that Jesus is Lord can stand on its own because the Triune God has declared it. As we taught the children to sing in children's Bible Clubs, "God said it. I believe it. And that settles that." It's a done deal. Drop the mic. This is solid irrefutable theology.

The Apostolic Tradition preaches and proclaims Jesus is Lord. The early church Fathers declared Jesus is Lord in the Creeds. The Ancient Rule of Faith of the Church has affirmed Jesus is Lord. Most convincingly of all is, God the Father, God the Son and God the Holy Spirit, the Three-in-One Godhead has placed the title of Lordship of all upon Jesus of Nazareth. But what kind of Lord is He?

King David, in Psalm 103, gives us a wonderful insight into what kind of Lord He is. He is the Lord . . .

- who forgives all your iniquity,

- who heals all your diseases,

- who redeems your life from the pit,

- who crowns you with steadfast love and mercy,

- who satisfies you with good so that your youth is renewed like the eagle's.

- who works righteousness and justice for all who are oppressed.

- who is merciful and gracious, slow to anger and abounding in steadfast love.

- who will not always chide, nor will he keep his anger forever.

- who does not deal with us according to our sins, nor repay us according to our iniquities.

This is the kind of Lord we need personally, for deep inside the secret chambers of our heart we feel and cry out like the saints and prophets of old:

- "I heard the sound of you in the garden, and I was afraid, because I was naked, and I hid myself" (Adam).

- "For I know my transgressions, and my sin is ever before me. Against you, you only, have I sinned and done what is evil in your sight, so that you may be justified in your words and blameless in your judgment" (King David).

- "Woe is me! For I am lost; for I am a man of unclean lips, and I dwell in the midst of a people of unclean lips" (Isaiah).

- "Depart from me, for I am a sinful man, O Lord" (Peter).

- "The saying is trustworthy and deserving of full acceptance, that Christ Jesus came into the world to save sinners, of whom I am the foremost" (Paul the Apostle).

There is no Lord like our Lord. We would be doomed to an eternal dark separation of anguish and pain for all eternity if it were not for the kindness, grace, and mercy of our Lord. He is worthy to be blessed, praised, and worshipped.

But what about in the context of missions? What kind of Lord is He that we can take full confidence, never shrinking back, knowing the surety of who He is declared to be as Lord in this spiritual war we find ourselves engaged in daily, hourly, and sometimes minute-by-minute? This is a critical question to answer as it will dictate how and if the Church will keep moving forward in missions.

The primary motif of Scripture is a warfare motif. From Genesis 3.14-15 to Revelation 20.7-10, and everything in between, the Bible unfolds this motif of conflict and conquest between the Kingdom of God and the Kingdom of Satan. When the Church sees the "war" for what it really is, then everyone will want to play their part. The clearer the Church sees the conflict and Jesus as Christus Victor, she will move forward in missions as priests of the Most High God, never shrinking back. To have a clear picture of what kind of Lord Jesus is in the context of missions we must look through the prism of this warfare motif. What is the *purpose*, *priority*, and *plan* of these two Kingdoms' governments, that are in conflict? Once we understand this, we can take a look at the Lord of missions with confidence and move forward to multiply.

The *purpose* of each kingdom is to rule and reign. The Almighty God, the Sovereign Creator of all things seen and unseen, is the rightful supreme ruler. Satan's attempted seizure of power (Isa. 14.13-14) in a time before our time, led to his expulsion from God's Kingdom domain and rule. He was expelled from the heavenlies and claimed the earth as his domain as the "prince of the power of the air." As a prince he tempted Jesus to relinquish his rule and reign when he, "took him up and showed him all the kingdoms of the world in a moment of time, and said to him,

'To you I will give all this authority and their glory, for it has been delivered to me, and I give it to whom I will. If you, then, will worship me, it will all be yours.' And Jesus answered him, 'It is written, " 'You shall worship the Lord your God, and him only shall you serve' (Luke 4:5-8)." Though the kingdoms of the world have been given over to Satan, we know the final outcome of this conflict. A day, a great and glorious day is coming, and all will hear the thunderous voices in heaven saying, "The kingdom of the world has become the Kingdom of our Lord and of His Christ and He shall reign forever and ever (Revelation 11:15)" for "the government shall be upon His shoulder (Isaiah 9:6)."

The *priority* of both these Kingdoms that are in conflict, are for the souls of humanity. Genesis 14 records the story of nine kingdoms at war with each other, four kings against five, and a great battle in the valley of Siddim (that is, the Salt Sea). An otherwise insignificant story except if it were not for Lot, the nephew of Abram, being taken prisoner along with all the spoils of war and the first record of Melchizedek, both king and priest connected with Jerusalem. Abram sets out with his fighting forces, secures the victory and, "Then he brought back all the possessions, and also brought back his kinsman Lot with his possessions, and the women and the people (Genesis 14:16)." We then come across an intriguing interaction that Abram has with this mystery Priest and King of the Most High God, Melchizedek, and the King of Sodom:

> And Melchizedek king of Salem brought out bread and wine. (He was priest of God Most High.) And he blessed him and said, "Blessed be Abram by God Most High, Possessor of heaven and earth; and blessed be God Most High, who has delivered your enemies into your hand!" And Abram gave him a tenth of everything. And the king of Sodom said to Abram, "Give me the persons, but take the goods for yourself." But Abram said to the king of Sodom, "I have lifted my hand to the Lord, God Most High, Possessor of heaven and earth,

that I would not take a thread or a sandal strap or anything
that is yours, lest you should say, 'I have made Abram rich.'"

~ Genesis 14.18-23

By translation, Melchizedek means, King of Righteousness. He is
also King of Salem, that is, King of peace. Here we have a shadowy
picture of the one who is our righteousness (1 Cor. 1.30) and
our peace (Eph. 2.14). The writer to the Hebrew followers of Jesus
said that Melchizedek, "is without father or mother or genealogy,
having neither beginning of days nor end of life, but resembling
the Son of God he continues a priest forever" (Heb. 7.3). This
Priest of God Most High offers Abram bread and wine as refreshment
to his body, which he receives. It was a foretaste of a coming
refreshment of souls seeking salvation, hope, and restoration of
fellowship with The Most High God. "But when the fullness of
time had come, God sent forth his Son, born of woman, born under
the law, to redeem those who were under the law, so that we
might receive adoption as sons" (Gal. 4.4-5). It was this same
Jesus, our righteousness and peace who, "took bread, and
when he had given thanks, he broke it and gave it to them,
saying, 'This is my body, which is given for you. Do this in
remembrance of me.' And likewise, the cup after they had eaten,
saying, 'This cup that is poured out for you is the new covenant
in my blood'" (Luke 22.19-20). What a fitting future picture of the
Lord Jesus instituting the Lord's supper as a remembrance of His
body (bread) and blood (wine) being given for our redemption
and reconciliation of our souls. Like the bread and wine given
to Abram for refreshment of body, so Jesus is our refreshment to
our soul. Abram, in return, gives Melchizedek a tenth of everything
as an offering of his gratefulness. We too, after receiving salvation
in Christ, give back to God our lives as a living sacrifice (Rom. 12.1).
This living sacrifice is to the very point where, "I have been
crucified with Christ. It is no longer I who live, but Christ who
lives in me. And the life I now live in the flesh I live by faith in
the Son of God, who loved me and gave himself for me" (Gal. 2.20).

Following this beautiful picture of the Christ of Redemption, we have the king of Sodom stepping up and entering the conversation. No name is given to him. All we know is he is the king of that city whose sin was so grave that it rose to the very heights of God. What a fitting representation of Satan and his Kingdom of Darkness. As a king, he has a right to receive all that is rightfully his. In gratitude, the king of Sodom, offers a "gift" of thanks to Abram, "Give me the persons, but take the goods for yourself." The Hebrews translation for persons are souls. This interaction between Melchizedek and the king of Sodom with Abram is a shadow of what takes place in the supernatural world. Satan wants to keep souls. I believe he would gladly give up all the "goods", i.e., the treasures of this world, to keep souls under his "lock and key." In his craftiness he plays his trump card, the goods of this world, in order to gain an advantage to retaining souls in his clutches. But it's a trump card – "a valuable resource that may be used, especially as a surprise, in order to gain an advantage" (Oxford Languages). Abram refused to take the bait. We too, who follow in the footsteps of the faith of Abraham, and as ambassadors of the Kingdom of God, must see the trump card for what it is and keep our eyes on souls.

We now come to *the plan* of each kingdom. How do these two kingdoms intend to battle for the souls of people in this spiritual cosmic conflict? Is the strategic plan of action of each kingdom the same? No. God's plan for the expansion of His Kingdom, His rule and reign, for the liberation and rescue of souls, has been initiated in His Son (John 3.16). Jesus was (Gen. 3.15), is (Acts 4.11-12), and always will be (Rev. 21.6-7) the Plan of God. Jesus is Plan A and there is no Plan B. Jesus, in whom God is well pleased (Matt. 3.7), is the plan that, "can open the eyes of the spiritually blind; can turn those in darkness towards the light; can liberate from the power of Satan to God, that they may receive forgiveness of sins and a place among those who are sanctified by faith in Jesus" (Acts 26.18). Jesus is the one-and-only who has "torn the veil" (Matt. 27.51) that separated us sinners from the presence of the Holy God. This tearing asunder has now given us a new and living way (Heb. 10.20) into the presence of God Almighty.

2 Corinthians 2.11 says that we do not need to be outwitted by Satan and are not to be ignorant of his designs. Satan's plan, his objective and chief aim is simple: nullify, cancel, blind, mute God's Plan A, the saving power of the Gospel. "In their case the god of this world has blinded the minds of unbelievers, to keep them from seeing the light of the gospel of the glory of Christ who is the image of God" (2 Cor. 4.4). He is the tempter who seeks through affliction to turn believers away from the gospel (1 Thess. 3.5), to hinder God's servants in their ministry to proclaim the Gospel (1 Thess. 2.18), who raises up false apostles to pervert the truth of the gospel (2 Cor. 11.14), and at times silences the voice of God's heralds of the Gospel (Acts 7.54–60). This is Satan's main objective. He will do all he can to frustrate God's Plan A of redemption in Jesus Christ and will continue this plan to the end of the age when he will incarnate himself in the man of lawlessness (2 Thess. 2.4-10).

We are born into the "mother of all conflicts" and none can escape it. John Dawson in *Taking Our Cities for God*, said, "According to the Bible, our lives are lived in the midst of an invisible spiritual war. One of the most dangerous things we can do is simply ignore this reality." Jesus saw past the temporal outer man and saw the unseen spiritual realty that all of humanity was harassed (Greek – to fillet alive; to skin) and helpless (Matt. 9.36). The soul of every person is a battleground of tragic conflict between the Kingdom of God and the Kingdom of Darkness. Considering this reality, we can now answer the question, what kind of Lord is Jesus?

"The Lord is a man of war; the Lord is His name" (Exod. 15.3). This "man of war" leads the angelic armies of heaven. They follow His lead (Rev. 19.14). In Roman times, an army was made up of 28 legions and a legion constituted 4,000–6,000 soldiers. During the betrayal and arrest of Jesus in the Garden of Gethsemane, when swords were drawn for battle, Jesus puts a stop to potential death and chaos and states, "Do you think that I cannot appeal to my Father, and he will at once send me more than twelve legions of angels?" (Matt. 26.53). Jesus had the authority to command 48,000–72,000 angels to descend upon the small plot of garden ground. And to think that one of these angels of the Lord, "went out and put to death a hundred and eighty-five thousand in the Assyrian camp when they were encamped around Mount Zion/ The City of Peace/Jerusalem" (2 Kings 19.35). Jesus is not who you imagine Him to be but who He declares Himself to be and He has declared Himself to be "a man of war."

God, through the Holy Spirit, has chosen to reveal Himself to us in words and pictures that we can grasp in our finite minds. Some we cling to more than others. *The Lord is a Warrior* is not one that most of the Church wants to adopt. A warrior is violent, bloody, decisive, relentless, aggressive. But this is exactly the imagery/reality we need when we think about the evil destructive forces that are at work in this world. We need a Warrior who we serve in missions.

When Jesus entered our humanity as a babe wrapped in swaddling clothes, lying in a manger, it was in disguise. His first coming fooled the demonic forces of darkness. They knew who He was, but they didn't know why He had entered into their domain. "Ha! What have you to do with us, Jesus of Nazareth? Have you come to destroy us? I know who you are—the Holy One of God" (Luke 4.34). But they were wrong. It wasn't yet the time of their demise. Jesus had entered as, "the Lamb of God, who takes away the sin of the world!" (John 1.29).

The Lamb of God who suffered and died, rose from the dead as the Victorious Warrior. He has "disarmed the rulers and authorities and put them to open shame, by triumphing over them in him" (Col. 2.15). Jesus was a literal Trojan Horse, that is, he came secretly to undermine Satan and his kingdom and destroy his works (1 John 3.8). The Lord, the "man of war," went in disguise into Satan's domain, bound him, and plundered souls (Matt. 12.29) to set the captives free (Luke 4.18). The chains of oppression and humiliation have been shattered by this Warrior, this Man of War. The Lord, who has been given all authority and power, now calls all of humanity to "COME FORTH" (John 11.43). All who respond and submit to His salvation and Lordship, are welcomed, and received into His Kingdom under His banner.

John the Revelator gives us an incredible insight into the Lord's return when He will set up the visible Kingdom in perfect righteousness, peace, and joy (Rom. 14.17), "Then I saw heaven opened, and behold, a white horse! The one sitting on it is called Faithful and True, and in righteousness he judges and makes war. His eyes are like a flame of fire, and on his head are many diadems, and he has a name written that no one knows but himself. He is clothed in a robe dipped in blood, and the name by which he is called is The Word of God. And the armies of heaven, arrayed in fine linen, white and pure, were following him on white horses. From his mouth comes a sharp sword with which to strike down the nations, and he will rule them with a rod of iron. He will tread the winepress of the fury of the wrath of God the Almighty. On his robe and on his thigh he has a name written, King of kings and Lord of lords" (Rev. 19.11-16). The Lord Jesus is frightening. He is not one to be played around with. He will come to judge and make war with the armies of heaven following Him. It is a terrible and fearful sight as He comes to exact the wrath of God Almighty on all who would not "COME FORTH" and submit to His rule and reign as the risen Lord.

These three words, Jesus is Lord, have dismantled Satan and his domain of darkness. Though Satan is the prince of the power of the air (Eph. 2.2), all the authority in heaven and earth have been given to Jesus (Matt. 28.18). He is *Christus Victor*, the triumphant One over all the evil powers that have infiltrated this good earth (Gen. 1). Satan's wrath and vile has been poured out though, "for the devil has come down to you in great wrath, because he knows that his time is short" (Rev. 12.12b). Yes, his time is short. Martin Luther stated it well in his great hymn, *A Mighty Fortress Is Our God*:

> And though this world, with devils filled,
> Should threaten to undo us,
> We will not fear, for God has willed
> His truth to triumph through us.
> The prince of darkness grim,
> We tremble not for him;
> His rage we can endure,
> For lo! his doom is sure;
> One little word shall fell him.

One word from the Lord Jesus will be the end of Satan and his works of evil and destruction. Until then, there are forces of evil that must be put down. We must move forward in missions for the billions of souls bound, helpless, and hopeless in the Kingdom of Darkness. Our confidence to move forward aggressively in missions comes in being confident of this one fact that, "The Lord is a man of war; the Lord is His name."

Content 2: "E" of an Apostolic Missions Platform: *Endearment*

Since Jesus is Lord, our foundational action for our *Apostolic Missions Platform* is to be endeared to Jesus. We endear ourselves to Christ not for the sake of missions but for Christ alone. He is Lord, and as Lord, requires our full devotion. The great missionary to the Gentiles, Paul the Apostle, made this the chief aim of his life. "But whatever gain I had, I counted as loss for the sake of Christ. Indeed, I count everything as loss because of the surpassing worth of knowing Christ Jesus my Lord. For his sake I have suffered the loss of all things and count them as rubbish, in order that I may gain Christ and be found in him, not having a righteousness of my own that comes from the law, but that which comes through faith in Christ, the righteousness from God that depends on faith, that I may know him and the power of his resurrection, and may share his sufferings, becoming like him in his death, that by any means possible I may attain the resurrection from the dead" (Phil. 3.7-11).

To be endeared to Jesus is the foundation and truly the whole of Christianity. It is in a league of its own. It is the first "E" in our *Apostolic Missions Platform.* "In Him we live and move and have our being" (Acts 17.28). "He is the image of the invisible God, the firstborn of all creation. For by him all things were created, in heaven and on earth, visible and invisible, whether thrones or dominions or rulers or authorities – all things were created through him and for him. And he is before all things, and in him all things hold together. And he is the head of the body, the church. He is the beginning, the firstborn from the dead, that in everything he might be preeminent" (Col. 1.15-18).

As Lord who has been given all authority, Jesus makes it very clear what is to be rendered, given, to Him. In Matthew 22.15-22 it says, "Then the Pharisees went and plotted how to entangle him in his words. And they sent their disciples to him, along with the Herodians, saying, 'Teacher, we know that you are true and teach the way of God truthfully, and you do not care about anyone's opinion, for you are not swayed by appearances. Tell us, then, what you think. Is it lawful to pay taxes to Caesar, or not?' But Jesus, aware of their malice, said, 'Why put me to the test, you hypocrites? Show me the coin for the tax.' And they brought him a denarius. And Jesus said to them, 'Whose likeness and inscription is this?' They said, 'Caesar's.' Then he said to them,

'Therefore render to Caesar the things that are Caesar's, and to God the things that are God's.' When they heard it, they marveled, and they left him and went away."

Jesus looks at a coin and asks his questioners whose image is on the coin, and they answer, "Caesar's." Jesus's reply is to render, or give back, to Caesar the coin since his image is branded on the coin. The obvious question then, is, "Whose likeness and inscription are on us?" God Himself answers the question, "Let us make man in our image; after our likeness" (Gen. 1.26a). If God's image and likeness is inscribed on us, then we must render ourselves to God, that is, give back to God ourselves since his image is branded on us. Endearment to the Lord Jesus is rendering to Him what is rightfully His.

The phrase, "Who you are is more important than what you do" is a true statement. Activity cannot be a replacement for intimacy with Jesus. In fact, this is the foundation upon which all our activity, our identity, and our purpose is formed. John 15:5, "I am the vine; you are the branches. Whoever abides in me and I in him, he it is that bears much fruit, for apart from me you can do nothing." Abiding in Christ is being filled with the Spirit and being filled with the Spirit is abiding in Christ.

Endearment was the way of the Apostles, "Now when they saw the boldness of Peter and John, and perceived that they were uneducated, common men (the Greek word used is idiotai from which we get the word, idiot), they were astonished. And they recognized that they had been with Jesus" (Acts 4.13). Anyone, male or female, rich or poor, slave or free, young, or old, "red, yellow, black, or white" who endear themselves to Jesus have common spiritual roots in Peter and John – idiots for Jesus. That endearment alone is all that is needed to shake the foundations of the forces of darkness, for when the disciples went out in "idiot pairs", they came back and said, "Lord, even the demons are subject to us in your name!" (Luke 10.17b).

Celsus, a second century Alexandrian intellectual wrote this about Christianity, "Far from us, say the Christians, be any man possessed of any culture, or wisdom or judgement; their aim is to convince only worthless and contemptible people, idiots, slaves, poor women and children . . . they would not dare to address an audience of intellectual men . . . but if they see a group of young people or slaves or rough folk, there they push themselves in and seek to win the admiration of the crowd" (Stephen Neill, *A History of Christian Mission*, New York: Penguin Books, 1974, p. 45). Like the early Christians, we must be convinced that God has chosen the poor, marginalized, least of these to expand and advance His Kingdom to every people group on earth. The poor are the next wave of "Kingdom foot soldiers, ambassadors, priests" in God's kingdom advancement into "enemy occupied territory." The Church must believe and expect great things from the poor.

Are you so endeared to Jesus, that the saved and the unsaved smell His sweet aroma upon your life? "But thanks be to God, who in Christ always leads us in triumphal procession, and through us spreads the fragrance of the knowledge of him everywhere. For we are the aroma of Christ to God among those who are being saved and among those who are perishing, to one a fragrance from death to death, to the other a fragrance from life to life. Who is sufficient for these things?" (2 Cor. 2.14-16).

Do the demonic forces know about you because of your endearment to Jesus? The seven sons of Sceva weren't endeared to Jesus and it cost them their blood, their clothes, and their pride. "Then some of the itinerant Jewish exorcists undertook to invoke the name of the Lord Jesus over those who had evil spirits, saying, "I adjure you by the Jesus whom Paul proclaims." Seven sons of a Jewish high priest named Sceva were doing this. But the evil spirit answered them, "Jesus I know, and Paul I recognize, but who are you?" And the man in whom was the evil spirit leaped on them, mastered all of them and overpowered them, so that they fled out of that house naked and wounded" (Acts 19.13-16). Being the sons of a high priest, probably meant they were moral, ethical, upright, respected, and adhered to the law. This holds no power though in the spiritual realm. Jesus as Lord is the authority and power. Being endeared to Him, is why and how we can move forward in missions. The evil spirit recognized Paul because Paul's life was endeared to Christ. "For to me to live is Christ, and to die is gain" (Phil. 1.21).

Being endeared to Jesus is a simple thing and yet it is probably the most difficult thing. Our spiritual enemy will do all he can to distract you from devoting (to hang out with) time to the Lord Jesus. As Screwtape admonished his nephew Wormwood, in C. S. Lewis's *The Screwtape Letters*, on how to make the Patient interested in other movements, ". . . the safest road to hell is the gradual one – the gentle slope, soft underfoot, without sudden turnings, without milestones, without signposts," so the enemy works today. He works gradually using a gentle slope of subtle lies that cause compromises, this day and then the next, and before you know it one has slipped away from a disciplined endearment to Jesus. Paul warned the Corinthians about the enemy's tactic when he said, "But I am afraid that as the serpent deceived Eve by his cunning, your thoughts will be led astray from a sincere and pure devotion to Christ" (2 Cor. 11.3).

Endearment is a fight, a battle. It is discipline that you must work at, "Therefore, my beloved, as you have always obeyed, so now, not only as in my presence but much more in my absence, work out your own salvation with fear and trembling, for it is God who works in you, both to will and to work for his good pleasure" (Phil. 2.12-13). A disciplined devotion to Jesus is not meant to be a restraint but is for our benefit. The Apostle Paul exhorted the Corinthians in this, "I say this for your own benefit, not to lay any restraint upon you, but to promote good order and to secure your undivided devotion to the Lord" (1 Cor. 7.35). This devotion must be rooted deep inside of you. It is a serious call to a devout and holy life. The seed of the root is the certainty that Jesus is Lord. All power and authority have been given to Him (Matt. 28.18) and his Kingdom is unshakeable (Heb. 12.28).

Let me make it clear. Though this is a book on missions with the mandate of our Lord to go and keep moving forward, missions is not the Christians first duty nor the chief end of man. To be and to do are both action words that are integral to life. What a man is comes first in the sight of God, "Let us make man in our own image" (Gen. 1.26). We were created to be like God. We then were given a responsibility to do: "Be fruitful and multiply and fill the earth and subdue" (Gen. 1.28). The Fall changed who we were created and intended to be. Our nature, our very heart, became corrupt which then corrupted what we did. God saw the cause of man's wicked ways and that "every imagination of the thoughts of his heart was only evil continually." "The stream of our doing now flows out of a fountain polluted by evil thoughts and imaginations."

The fountain needed to be sanctified in order that our doing would be good and pleasing to God. We needed a new nature if we were to do anything of good for that is what we were created for, "For we are His workmanship, created in Christ Jesus for good works, which God prepared beforehand, that we should walk in them" (Eph. 2.10). Our being and doing are related. It is a cause-and-effect relationship. The primary work of the Holy Spirit is to restore the lost soul to intimate fellowship with God through the conviction of sin, righteousness, and judgment (John 16.8). Those who respond in faith to God's redemption in Christ are reconciled to God and become a new creation (2 Cor. 5.17). The Holy Spirit then leads the willing heart of the new creation into deeper communion and active missions. The willing heart is the one who purposefully seeks to draw near and be endeared to Christ.

Though the Apostle Paul counted all things as loss compared to being endeared to the Lord Jesus, he worked harder than all the other Apostles (I Cor. 15.10). Endearment doesn't mean seclusion or missions inactivity. The closer we get to the Lord Jesus the clearer we hear His heartbeat. "For God so loved the world that He gave is one and only Son," is the beat of the rhythm of His heart. This rhythm becomes our rhythm and like Paul we cry out, "For Christ's love compels us, because we are convinced that one died for all, and therefore all died. And he died for all, that those who live should no longer live for themselves but for him who died for them and was raised again" (2 Cor. 5.14-15). All our activity, identity, direction, fruitfulness will flow out of our devotion to abide in the Lord Jesus who is the Lord of the Harvest.

The world, the flesh, and the enemy seek to draw us away from this *Apostolic Missions Platform* for the source of life and missions and to find it in other people, places, or things. The Spirit only does what he hears and sees Jesus doing. Do not think you can participate in missions apart from your endearment to the Lord Jesus. Fight for this. "Draw near to God and He will draw near to you" (James 4.8).

Connection:
Rules of Engagement (ROE)

If you were looking from the outside-in, it was a strange looking scene: A young white guy, blonde hair, and blue eyes, 130 pounds at 5'9½" (almost 5'10"), with boundless energy running back-and-forth on the court playing mid-night basketball with gang guys that I would pick up from the mean streets in the "Devil's Half-Mile," the community where Susan and I lived. To say the least, I was completely out of place. The life and world view of these gang guys was as opposite in direction as the North Pole is from the South Pole. I don't even have any tattoos or scars (bullet or knife).

How was I to connect with them? God had to remind me of a deeper truth through the words of one of the gang guys. "Bob. You don't know anything about us [sprinkled with expletives]." Basically, he was saying that I'm uneducated and common; an "idiot." "But we know that you love us. You're not a phony. Jesus is real to you." The deeper truth God taught me was my endearment to Jesus is all I need for others to see Jesus.

Apostolic Missions Platform Response: Metrics for Church Planters

I. *Can the potential church planter feed themselves spiritually?*

Can they survive in the "battlefield" when the battle is raging and they have run out of "rations" – money, job, vehicles (broken and stolen), been robbed, health, physical threats and experiences, family struggles and sacrifices, sleep, let alone the constant lies and attacks from the devil and his minions (I write from experience)? When everything runs out can the potential planter retreat into their prayer closet and find and eat upon the bread and blood of Jesus for sustenance and life (John 6.52-57)? No one can take Jesus away from you except yourself. By that, I mean, one is either disciplined or not to endear themselves to Jesus through the daily disciplines. It doesn't matter if the planter is in Mongolia or Massachusetts, in the slums of Nairobi or the slopes of Beverly Hills. Every disciple of Jesus is to move towards maturity in Christ. Instead of others giving you spiritual milk in a "spiritual baby bottle" they move to feeding themselves. How much more the individual who feels they are being called to enter enemy-occupied territory to establish an outpost of the Kingdom of God? This is a must in our church planter assessment process. The one abiding in Christ (John 5:1-5) knows how to "eat the flesh" and "drink the blood" of Jesus each day just as any person knows how to make a meal each day in which to receive strength and nourishment.

II. *Those assessing church planters must be able to "see" that they have been with Jesus.*

Is their endearment to the Lord a sincere and pure devotion? Are they without any guile (a person of innocence, honest intent, and pure motives, whose life reflects the simple practice of conforming his daily actions to principles of integrity)? Is the aroma of the Lord Jesus upon him/her? Do you sense the righteousness, joy and peace of the Kingdom of God reigning in their life through the Holy Spirit? If you don't sense this in your spirit, or see it in their life, then the individual is not ready to be sent out into missions. They may be a John Mark who will be useful later but is not ready now. They will bring harm to the church planting effort just like the team of the Seven Sons of Sceva. We must know for certain that the potential planter has "been with Jesus" because our enemy will surely know if they are or are not (Acts 19).

III. *Is the rule and reign of the Lord and His Kingdom in the thoughts and actions of the potential church planter?*

When your emerging leader of your first church plant (1997) is extradited to Texas for murder, is Jesus Lord? When the 1992 Rodney King riots are raging in your community, is Jesus still on His sovereign throne in your life? Is the Lordship of Jesus so rooted and established in the potential planter that when the inevitable onslaughts of the Kingdom of Darkness hit the planter from the left and right, inside and outside, they will not abandon the Lord's calling but faithfully move forward because He is Lord? When Jesus is firmly established as Lord, the church planters prayer during the hard times is, "Let this cup pass from me. Nevertheless, not what I want but your will be done. I'm not shrinking back. Though I don't understand it, You rule and reign in this situation."

IV. Is there an unwavering confidence in the Lordship of Jesus in their life?

The Lordship of Jesus is critical to the enterprise of missions. There is no missions apart from the Lord Jesus. If there is the faintest of doubts to the Lordship of Jesus in the church planter, the demonic realm will make folly of the planter and of the effort. Those who are assessing our church planters, must know with absolute confidence and conviction that the one they are appointing, and authorizing have submitted every area of their life to the Lord. The responsibility rests on the sending authority.

Apostolic Missions Platform Response: *Endearment*

As Lord of all things visible and invisible, Jesus can do whatever He wants, whenever He wants, with whomever He wants, and however He wants to do it. This absolutely applies to missions as He is the Lord of the Harvest. There are times in which the Lord will break through the natural order of things to work the supernatural as only He determines and understands. More often though, He does work through the natural laws of our world which means He works through the laws of preparation. No newborn hits the ground running the 100-yard dash in ten seconds. There are laws of preparation to get to that point – crawling, standing, waddling, walking, jogging, running, training, racing that require one to be disciplined.

Don't be deceived. Endearment here is not meant to be a soft, warm, comfy-cozy word. It is a rough, self-discipline of the heart, soul, strength, and mind in which the Lord will rightfully demand your all. It is not for delicate, brittle saints. It is for those women and men who unite with Paul the Apostle, who was martyred for the Lord while engaged in missions, and will count everything as loss because of the surpassing worth of knowing Christ Jesus their Lord (Phil. 3.8); who willingly will suffer the loss of all things and count them as rubbish, in order that they may gain Christ (Phil. 3.8); who will share in his sufferings, becoming like him in his death, that by any means possible they may attain the resurrection from the dead (Phil. 3.10-11); who strain and press forward towards the goal for the prize of the upward call of God in Christ Jesus (Phil. 3.14); who, because of their maturity, are constantly thinking this way (Phil. 3.15). Endearment to the Lord Jesus necessitates an abhorrence of evil (Rom. 12.9), a denying of self (Matt. 16.24), fleeing from evil (1 Thess. 5.22), and to not befriend the world (James 4.4).

Jude 1.21 says, "keep yourselves in the love of God, waiting for the mercy of our Lord Jesus Christ that leads to eternal life." Do you know how to keep yourself in the love of God? To be endeared to Christ? Here are several foundational preparations you can discipline yourself in, whether called to missions (the sending forth of authorized persons to unchurched communities to proclaim the Gospel in order to win converts to Jesus Christ, make disciples from the converts, and gather together the disciples to form functioning, multiplying local churches, that bear the fruit of the Kingdom of God in that community) or not. I have found the simplicity of these disciplines to be instrumental in my years of missions "from and for" the poor. They have kept me moving forward to multiply.

1. *Discipline yourself in the Church's Sacred Roots* (Shorthand term for "Great Tradition," *Sacred Roots: A Primer on Retrieving the Great Tradition* by Dr. Don Davis).

   The Christian faith is anchored on the person and work of Jesus of Nazareth, the Lord, whose incarnation, crucifixion, and resurrection, and ascension forever changed the invisible and visible world. In the Church's early years, she grew from a small, persecuted minority to a Kingdom movement expanding and advancing to "the ends of the earth." The sacred roots that the early Church produced gave us our worship (the theology and liturgy of Baptism and Communion), our theology (Canon and confession - the major creeds of the Church, and the central tenets of the Faith), spiritual formation (discipleship and Church leadership), and witness (missions and ministry). Each year, The Urban Ministry Institute community, of which I am a part, deliberately shares a spiritual quest and journey, to seek the Lord together in Scripture. This practice informs our commitment to walking the Christ life according to the rhythms of the Church year. Commit to participate in the TUMI Annual (*www.tumiannual.com*) where we:

a. *Refresh ourselves daily with the Story of God.* This discipline of daily scriptural reading rehearses God's redemptive plan for humanity's salvation and the inbreaking of His Kingdom (the rule and reign of God) in the person and mission of the One "He loves and is well pleased" (Matt. 3.17), Jesus of Nazareth. We now live in the Age of the Church, the advancement and expansion of God's Kingdom rule and reign, but earnestly look towards the Age to Come, when God acts in power to destroy His enemies and save His people. It is the future visible realm of God's Kingdom in which His children, those who in obedient faith are adopted into His family, will enjoy the fullness of His blessings for eternity. Though we are not eyewitnesses to the life and ministry of Jesus like the apostles, those preparing for missions should know the life and ministry of Jesus as though they were an eyewitness.

This daily discipline allows you to read through the
Bible at least once a year. Less than 15% of Christians
have read through the Bible, the Story of God. As
people of The Story, I would think we would want to
immerse ourselves in the Story like the man that
evangelist Robert L. Sumner talks about in his book,
The Wonders of the Word of God. A man in Kansas
City was severely injured in an explosion. The victim's
face was badly disfigured, and he lost his eyesight as
well as both hands. He was just a new Christian, and
one of his greatest disappointments was that he could
no longer read the Bible.

Then he heard about a lady in England who read
Braille with her lips. Hoping to do the same, he sent
for some books of the Bible in Braille. Much to his
dismay, however, he discovered that the nerve endings
in his lips had been destroyed by the explosion. One
day, as he brought one of the Braille pages to his lips,
his tongue happened to touch a few of the raised
characters, and he could feel them. Like a flash he
thought, I can read the Bible using my tongue. At the
time Robert Sumner wrote his book, the man had
"read" through the entire Bible four times.

Last of all this discipline opens the door to hear from
the Holy Spirit as one meditates upon the daily
reading of the Scriptures.

b. *Engage in book reading.* Our book readings are
specifically related to the theme we are focusing on
during the liturgical year. The book readings are not
for the purpose of gaining knowledge as an end but
a means to strengthen and encourage our part in

the Story of God so that leaders are equipped, and movements empowered to expand and advance His Kingdom around the world.

2. *Discipline yourself for the purpose of godliness.*

It was said to me during my early years of missions, "Are you holy enough for the task." Yes, holiness is to be set apart by God. It is His calling and work and yet Paul the Apostle wrote to the Corinthians, "Since we have these promises, beloved, let us cleanse ourselves from every defilement of body and spirit, bringing holiness to completion in the fear of God" (2 Cor. 7.1). The Spirit of the Lord will not use an unholy, undisciplined vessel for His purposes. This is not a discipline for salvation. Our salvation is solely founded on Christ alone, our Cornerstone. We build upon this foundation to be available and ready to the Lord of the Harvest for honorable service.

The spiritual disciplines throughout Church history have assisted all disciples in cleansing themselves from every defilement of body and spirit. It is a life-long discipline of practicing fervently and regularly the personal and corporate disciplines. Here is a list that I have implemented in my life of godliness which has prepared me for the daily call of missions: Prayer, Meditate on God's Word, Fasting, Worship, Simplicity, Giving. There are other disciplines that saints and those engaged in missions have implemented into their life. Whatever you chose, it is to lead you into, "bringing holiness to completion" to be a vessel of honorable use that the Lord can use for missions and mission.

3. *Discipline yourself to a Church Community.*

As I mentioned earlier, there is no missions apart from the Church. Who else is going to know and assess the calling for missions upon an individual than the leadership of a local church who knows everything about the potential church planter (Acts 13:1-3)? They're going to know if they have "been with Jesus"; can "feed themselves spiritually upon the Lord Jesus;" have seen them unwavering in the Lordship of Jesus during the battle challenges of life; and can witness their godly life and faithfulness to the Church.

4. *Discipline yourself to create a personal library of Christian devotional classics.*

There have been a host of saints who have gone before us whose writings are timeless and a must read for any follower of Jesus who seeks a "sincere and pure devotion to Christ." I have a small, simple, library of devotional classics that I read over and over. There are nuggets I mine each time I read them. These are the books that the Holy Spirit uses to conform, reform, and transform my walk with Jesus as I journey to, "the city that has foundations, whose designer and builder is God" (Heb. 11.10).

Connection Story

It was 1982, my first year on staff. I moved into the Single Men's Home which was nestled in the African American section of Wichita, Kansas. I didn't know Tee well, like the other staff. In fact, I'm not sure if that was her birth certificate name. All I knew is that she was an elderly saint who took care of her invalid daughter who was bedridden for over forty years. She was small in stature and looked frail. Her home must have been less than 600 square feet and was unfit for living. One day I went over to visit Tee and to bring a new/used couch that had been donated to the ministry. When I lifted her old couch to remove it, countless cockroaches fell on my head and clothing. They were everywhere and in everything. The place should have been condemned and torn down. Though Tee lived a hard life, there was an inner joy that overflowed from within her life that most others would raise their fists to God and curse Him. Not Tee! She exemplified Paul's words to the Thessalonian Church, "give thanks in all circumstances; for this is the will of God in Christ Jesus for you" (1 Thess. 5.18). Though, I'm not sure she could read, she always had a Kingdom word of thankfulness to share with me. This saint, unknown but to very few, who lived in poverty, left a "rich" mark in my spirit. She lived a life of endearment to the Lord Jesus and was used by the Spirit of the Lord to begin shaping my *Apostolic Missions Platform*. I look forward to seeing this saint one day when walking streets of gold in the New Jerusalem.

Chapter 2

THE HOLY SPIRIT:
Empower

Key Old Testament Verse

The Spirit of the Lord speaks by me; His word is on my tongue.

~ 2 Samuel 23.2

Key New Testament Verse

But you will receive power when the Holy Spirit has come upon you, and you will be my witnesses in Jerusalem and in all Judea and Samaria, and to the end of the earth.

~ Acts 1.8

Contact: Situation Awareness

"Take some of the gang guys into the Sierras and camp out for several days and share the Gospel." "Are you sure about this Lord?" was my inner reply. "Camping? Gang guys? Okay. I'm on it."
It wasn't your typical "sing around the campfire" and toasting marshmallows experience. Despite the semi-automatics that some of the guys brought and other crazy situations, the guys respected me and on the last night quietly listened as I shared once again the good news of the love of God in Jesus for the

forgiveness of our sin. Later, I would bury one of them; one went to the psychiatric ward; one was sentenced to life in prison for triple homicide; and one went into the ministry. He became the first youth pastor of Bethany Inner City Church, my first church plant in partnership with Pastor Jonathan Villalobos.

"Go down to the Community Center to the meeting that is taking place tonight." The violence was drastically escalating in our low income/high crime community and there was a gathering of concerned people. My family lived here so it made sense to attend and voice my concern. It was a late-night meeting and when I walked into the center, I realized this might not be the best place for me to voice my concern as a white person, even though I lived here. The meeting was organized by the Nation of Islam. I couldn't see anything good coming out of this scenario. "Are you sure about this Lord?" Immediately, I was surrounded by two "sergeants-at-arms." Using some very choice expletives, within inches of my face, the two asked what I was doing here. As I was explaining that I was a pastor who lived in the community, a friend of mine walked in and stepped between them and said, "he's with me." Tony (not his real name) was once a Black Gangster Disciple but was now a Jesus Disciple. His is an amazing story of redemption that I had the joy of discipling as a follower of Jesus. Though the two sergeants-in-arms relented their verbal assaults and potential physical harm, I was commanded to "shut your mouth" and to "stand in the back corner." Tony represented our concerns as community members and Christians.

I was in South Central Los Angeles, doing "contact evangelism" when I noticed a group of African Americans dressed in camouflage, gathered in a corner park. The leader was speaking loudly but I was unable to understand what he was saying. As I drew near, I realized it was the Black Hebrew Israelites, a radical militant group. They were street preaching their antisemitic and anti-white hatred. "Go over there and share the Gospel with that group of

African Americans." "Are you sure about this Lord?" As we walked up to the group, my evangelism partner (who was Asian and also hated by them), and I were immediately encircled by several of the Black Hebrew Israelites. This group of "foot soldiers," dressed in camouflage, faced outwardly with their backs facing us. The leader of the group entered the circled and spewed his hate filled speech for thirty minutes in our faces. At the end of his tirade he screamed, "So what do you have to say about this, you #@&%?," which immediately opened the opportunity to share the Gospel.

The Nickerson Gardens housing project, in Watts, is the largest of its kind west of the Mississippi River. It is the birthplace to the Bounty Hunter Blood gang. "Go start a children's Bible Club in Nickerson Gardens." "Are you sure about this Lord?" I made plans and worked things out with the Director of the Community Center located in the heart of the projects. He was an elderly African American gentleman, whose face showed the heartache of violence, drugs, and gangs he must have seen and experienced. I could see the surprise and concern when I entered his office, but he was very grateful that we would do something like that for the children. The first day of children's Bible Club, while playing games, we noticed we were surrounded on the perimeter by gang members. They were all young, wearing their red bandanas and shades. The children didn't think anything of it, but the volunteers were nervous, and I needed to calm their fears. I walked over to who I thought was the leader. "Is everything okay?" He looked at me and said, "We're just protecting the children from any potential rival gang interference." "That's a relief," I thought. We talked a little more, though I can't remember what about, and then I went back to the Bible Club. The laughter and joy brought smiles to the moms hanging out the project windows. It was like they wished they could have joined in. We left encouraged and looked forward to the children's Bible Club opening up doors to the adult community and gang members. When we went back the next day, I noticed the Projects were eerily silent. I told everyone to stay in the van as I walked up to the door of the Center and knocked. The Director slowly opened one of the two metal doors. "What are you doing here? You must leave. It's not safe. When you left yesterday, members of the Crips came over. They shot and killed several of the Bloods. The Bloods are out for revenge and the area is locked down as it's going to get messy." He quickly thanked me for yesterday but urged me to leave right away. I heeded his words for our safety.

I could also talk about the Spirit speaking to me to start our first National Teen Retreat, or our Camp Adventure for youth and teens, the first Family Camp, the first Urban Church Association, the first Men's Retreat, moving to the East Coast to provide leadership and church planting efforts. From big things to small things my journey as His disciple has been one of, "Are you sure about this Lord?" This was the journey of Jesus as well. While in the Garden of Gethsemane he prayed, "My Father, if it be possible, let this cup pass from me" (Matt. 26.39a) or, "Are you sure about this Father?"

✔ ━━━━ Content 1
✔ ━━━━ Missions Plank: *The Holy Spirit*

✔ ━━━━
✔ ━━━━   I must confess that I have questioned the Spirit
✔ ━━━━   of the Lord countless times. "Are you sure about
      this Lord?" In church planting, it's not the
questioning that matters. It's what you do when you know the Spirit of the Lord is moving you forward through the questioning. I would look at the situation through my own thinking, fears, or inadequacies. And by the way, I think that is normal for any person. All of us struggle in some way or some area of life with the inner voice that daily whispers, "you're not good enough; look at you; who do you think you are; you're a nobody." It goes on and on and it never stops. But when a man or a woman comes to the obedient faith in Jesus Christ the Lord, he/she becomes a new creature (2 Cor. 5.17). The Holy Spirit is the One who then

gives the calling, gifting, anointing, and instruction in missions. He infuses us with Himself that we might have the power to obey His direction in missions and ministry. We now have within us the ability to cry out to the Father what Jesus Himself cried out, "nevertheless, not as I will, but as you will" (Matt. 26.39b). Whatever the Spirit of the Lord is prompting us to do, we can lean upon the wise words of Proverbs 3:5-6, "Trust in the Lord with all your heart and lean not on your own understanding. In all your ways acknowledge Him and He will make your paths straight."

Without the Holy Spirit and our absolute surrender to Him, there would be no missions.

1. It is the Holy Spirit who calls and gifts people for missions (Acts 13.2).

2. It is the Holy Spirt who empowers people for missions (Acts 1.8).

3. It is the Holy Spirit who guides and gives directions for missions (Acts 8.29; 16.6-7). The Great Commission verses (Matt. 28.19-20; Mark 16.15; Luke 24.47; John 20.22-23) reveal the Church's missionary duties. It sets forth the basic framework and essentials for our assignment in missions. We find our directions for missions not in the limitless, ever-growing, ever-changing needs as they appear to us. We find our directions for missions in the Great Commission. Here it is clearly defined and delineated through a charter, compass, and a plan.

    a. Charter (given by a Sovereign Power): All authority has been given to Jesus.

    b. Compass (North. South. East. West.): Go (all the world, all nations, all creation)

    c. Plan (Simple yet detailed proposal on what to do)

1) Proclaim (the Gospel, repentance for the forgiveness of sins)

2) Disciple converts.

3) Baptize

4) Teach obedience to Christ's commands.

4. It is the Holy Spirit who grants divine boldness for witness (Acts 4.13, 31).

5. It is the Holy Spirit who influences every dimension of the effective preaching ministry (Acts 4.6; Acts 6.10).

6. It is the Holy Spirit who gives the wisdom of God to speak clearly (John 16.13; 1 Cor. 2.13).

7. It is the Holy Spirit who convicts of sin, righteousness, and judgment (John 16.8).

8. It is by the Holy Spirit one is born again (John 3.5-8).

9. It is by the Holy Spirit one can say, "Jesus is Lord" (1 Cor. 12.3).

10. It is the Holy Spirit who makes elders to oversee churches (Acts 20.28).

These Scriptures alone declare the importance, the necessity of the Holy Spirit in missions. It is imperative that if the Church is to continue to move forward into enemy occupied territory, that the representatives of the Kingdom of God, who are authorized and released to establish Outposts of the Kingdom of God, be absolutely surrendered to the Holy Spirit. He is the source of empowerment. Though Scriptures are sufficient in and of themselves, meditate upon the words of what some others have contributed to this Apostolic missions plank, The Holy Spirit. Let their words sink deep within you, that the Holy Spirit would stir your spirit to some form of action that will strengthen your resolve for missions.

The fact that missions essentially is a ministry of the Holy Spirit is both a comfort and a challenge to us – a comfort in that we may trust Him fully to accomplish His work, a challenge in that only Spirit-filled people, Spirit-sanctioned means, and Spirit-approved methods can be used effectively in mission ministries.

~ G.W. Peters, *A Theology of Missions.*

The secret of saintliness (and service in missions) is not the destruction of the will but the submergence of it in the will of God.

~ A. W. Tozer, *Incredible Christian.*

Acts does not begin with "The Lord Jesus said, 'go'"; but with "Ye shall receive power, and ye shall be witnesses." . . . He speaks not of men who, being what they were, strove to obey the last orders of a beloved Master, but of men who, receiving a Spirit, were driven by that Spirit to act in accordance with the nature of that Spirit.

~ Roland Allen, *The Ministry of the Spirit.*

The Christian way is different: harder, and easier. Christ says, "Give me All. I don't want so much of your time and so much of your money and so much of your work: I want you. I have not come to torment your natural self, but to kill it. No half-measures are any good. I don't want to cut off a branch here and a branch there, I want to have the whole tree down. I don't want to drill the tooth, or crown it, or stop it, but to have it out. Hand over the whole natural self, all the desires which you think innocent as well as the ones you think wicked – the whole outfit. I will give you a new self instead. In fact, I will give you Myself: my own will shall become yours." This is the whole of Christianity. There is nothing else.

~ C. S. Lewis, *Mere Christianity.*

We have given too much attention to methods and to machinery and to resources, and too little to the Source of Power, the filling with the Holy Spirit.

~ J. Hudson Taylor

Until you are filled with the Holy Spirit, don't go. After you are filled with the Holy Spirit, don't stay.

~ P. J. Titus

And I believe in the Holy Ghost,
The Lord and Giver of Life,
Who proceedeth from the Father and the Son;
Who with the Father and Son together
Is worshipped and glorified.

~ The 318 Bishops of the Council of Nicea

Absolute surrender to the Holy Spirit is a non-negotiable in missions. He expects and demands all disciples of the Lord Jesus to "count everything as loss" (Phil. 3.8) and to be "crucified with Christ" (Gal. 2.20) so that we no longer live but Jesus lives in us. It's submitting our will to His will. We follow Christ's example and humbly submit our looming concerns and fears into our heavenly Father's secure hands.

This is the person whom the Holy Spirit can use. Believers whose wills are fully submitted become Spirit filled and enabled to move forward in missions. They can reproduce the maturity and faithfulness they have in Christ into others. They have pressed on towards maturity (Heb. 6.1-8). They have persisted in watching their own life and doctrine so closely so as not to be disqualified themselves but, in turn apprentice others towards the finish line (1 Tim. 4.16). They are Empowered by the Holy Spirit for missions, the second "E" of our *Apostolic Missions Platform*.

Content 2:
"E" of an Apostolic Missions Platform:
Empower

Though there is a great amount of focus on the work of the Holy Spirit in the individual Christian, there is the community side to the Holy Spirit as well. It was the risen and exalted Lord Jesus who gave the Holy Spirit to form a new people who would constitute the "Community of the Kingdom" in a locality. This community of believers are to faithfully, and aggressively, move forward to multiply. Through the called and recognized leadership of the church, individuals would be identified, and empowered - given authority - to go and form functioning, multiplying local churches, that would bear the fruit of the Kingdom of God, where there is no church. Planting churches is the fruit of a local church's efforts in missions.

If this is the fruit of the Church's prayers and labors, then we must be clear on what a church is so that we know when it is planted. Ask a hundred different people and you might get a hundred different answers. The Bible gives many descriptive words for the Church. Here is a sampling from the song, *The Church of the Living God in Jesus Christ.* The words are by Dr. Don Davis and Rev. Terry Cornett, and the music is by Dr. Don Davis.

> A people of God's possession,
> A Nation thru Messiah's blood,
> A Body of Christ's own members,
> A Temple where God is loved,
> We're an Army that stands in battle,
> The Branches of God's True Vine,
> We're the Church of the Living God,
> In Jesus Christ.

A Witness to all the nations, a City set on the hill,
A Flame that burns for Jesus,
A Dwelling where Abba lives,
We're the Flock of the Great Shepherd,
A Virgin and Christ's dear Bride,
We're the Church of the Living God
In Jesus Christ.

A Chosen and Holy Nation, a Kingdom of Royal Priests,
An Ark that saves God's people, a Fold for Jesus Sheep!
We're a Vineyard for God's Own Pleasure,
The Object of His Desire,
We're the Church of the Living God,
In Jesus Christ.

Of critical importance in empowering for church planting is that the church plant team and the church planting movement know exactly what a church is so that they know when the task is completed, i.e., a church has been planted. If this is not clear, then our spiritual enemy, who hates the Bride of Christ, has the advantage. He will subtly play upon the church plant teams lack of clarity and bring frustration, impotence and ultimately, kill the effort and movement.

The radical minimum "marks" of a church must be biblical and practical for the sake of the church plant team and the movement. The Apostle Paul apparently had his marks. How else could he confidently go to "every church" (Acts 14.23) unless he knew what constituted a church for him to go to?

Understanding these "marks" empowers the church plant team by bringing clarity to the call and task the Lord of the Harvest has given them. So, what are the irreducible marks of a church? In coaching many church planters who were planting in communities of poverty, I have communicated the following four marks in one form (word or phrase) or another. For our purposes, I will use the Sacred Roots descriptive words. It is the radical minimum in knowing when a church is planted yet knowing that the church will grow and mature.

1. *Worship*. The Sacraments of Baptism (Matt. 3.13-17; 28.19-20; Rom. 6.1-14) and The Lord's Supper (Matt. 22.2-14; 26.26-31; 1 Cor. 11.17-34; Rev. 19.6-9) are firmly established within the community of gathered believers. It is the dramatic retelling and reenacting of the story of God. Notice that I do not mention how often or how to perform the two sacraments. The radical minimum is that they are established. The church planter and their sending authority determine these within their shared spirituality.

2. *Spiritual Formation*. To move from a convert to a disciple of the Lord Jesus is a process. (I will talk more about this in chapter four.) Leadership within the community must also be recognized knowing that eventually some will be appointed as elders. Apparently, Paul's radical minimum was leaders, was disciples (baptized and obeying what Jesus commanded), who others followed and respected. Looking again at Acts 14.23, Paul went to every church (already established) to appoint elders. We also see this in Titus 1.5 where the Apostle directs Titus to finish up what he did not have the chance to finish, which was to appoint elders. In Paul's apostolic church planting call and work, he was okay with the radical minimum of leadership, but not content until elders were appointed. In our present-day church planting efforts, we should be okay that leadership has been recognized within the church, but not content until elders are appointed. In other words, there must be a credentialing process for called and gifted individuals to be recognized as shepherds of the community; those who will hold a position of responsibility and authority to

spiritually feed and protect the flock under their care. When planting in communities of poverty, it requires wisdom as to what that credentialing process looks like. It must not compromise the responsibility of the calling to defend what the Church has believed everywhere, always and by all and at the same time does not place a burden on the individual that is impossible for them to accomplish.

3. *Theology*. The foundational doctrines of the Church, our Great Tradition, are firmly established. The doctrinal issues and challenges were all settled by the early Church Fathers and were consolidated into the Creeds. These Creeds were easily memorized by the illiterate masses within the Church so that all believers could understand and defend what the apostles taught. Today we call it a Statement of Faith.

   The Word is being taught. From its inception and throughout history, the Church has devoted itself to the apostles teaching (Acts 2:42). Our New Testament is the recognized culmination of writings from the Apostles of the Lord Jesus. Spiritual growth and guidance for living within the Community of Believers as well as our interactions in the world, are fully and completely, without error (inerrancy), found in their writings.

4. *Witness*. The God of missions, who, "in these last days has spoken to us by His Son" (Heb. 1.2), now enlists His people to action. Since the Day of Pentecost, we are now in the Church Age, and God Almighty is accomplishing His eternal purpose to establish His Kingdom through her. Through our witness in word and deed of God's reconciling work through Jesus Christ, we move forward in order to expand and advance His rule and reign.

The harvest field is vast and complex when considering Jesus's Great Commission mandate to go to "the nations" (*ta ethne*: race; people who are joined by practicing similar customs or common culture), to disciple and then gather into Communities of the Kingdom. Having these four marks for the foundation of a church brings clarity to the planter and the movement, and it stops our enemy from infiltrating any confusion as to the task and its completion. One can say, when observing these four established marks in a gathering of any size and location, "there is a church." What these four marks also address is a strategic way to move forward in this mission field of lost souls. Let me explain by a simple analogy of comparing this to building a house.

The beginning and most critical step in building a house is to lay the foundation. Forms are put into place and cement must be properly mixed before it is poured into the frames. Before any framing and building occur upon the foundation, the cement must be cured, smooth, and without any cracks. In church planting, the church planter lays the foundation. He sets the spiritual forms in place and pours the spiritual cement into the forms. These spiritual forms and cement are the four marks of a church. Once the planter determines that the foundation (the four marks) is firmly established, that is, cured, smooth and without cracks, the nations (race; people of a common culture – language, customs, celebrations, etc.) can frame and build upon this foundation a "structure" that is culturally sensitive and relevant according to their cultural preferences.

To expand on this spiritual comparison, they can frame in different size rooms (mega, micro, simple, organic, etc.), put 2x4s at different lengths (meet once a week, three times a week, every other week, etc.), secure electrical outlets where they deem best (have a food pantry, a thrift store, provide legal aid, etc.), use different size drywall (sing hymns, listen to tape worship, have a band), texture, colors, etc. Everything in parentheses are non-absolutes of what makes a church. The four marks of a church are the foundation of a church that is planted. They are the absolutes that must not be compromised. The church planter is authorized and commissioned to plant the church, not a concept of what s/he wants the church to look like. Plant the church and one can grow a vision of the church.

Thinking and applying the four marks to church planting makes the vastness and complexity of missions to the nations, attainable. It does not compromise the radical minimum of a biblical Church; the culture is not dependent upon the planter because the "framing and building" supplies come from within the culture (Self-Supporting and Self-Governing); it is reproducible when we think of the Kingdom principle of multiplication, i.e., the culture can identify, equip and release their own church planters to lay the foundation of the four marks of a church (Self-Propagating); allows for church planting movements to retain fruit that will last through a shared spirituality, a common practice, and be culturally sensitive to all people groups that make up the harvest field. They can move with velocity.

The Apostle Paul was approximately three weeks in Thessalonica and planted a church. He surely didn't have the time to train in money management principles, provide a marriage conference, address slavery issues or injustice issues of the ruling government, or the many other things that make for growth and maturity as a follower of Jesus in every area of life. As important as these are, and many other issues of life, the Apostle Paul proclaimed the Gospel leading to churches, bona fide churches, built on a solid radical minimum foundation. He entrusted the expected growth and nurture of the disciples through Spirit filled leaders. Paul was able to "fire and maneuver" and keep moving forward with the Gospel. Church planting and church planting movements can move with velocity. It's not complicated.

Planting churches like this allows the poor to be empowered and to fully engage and join the Church in the Great Commission. To empower the poor, or anyone, in missions – "the sending forth of authorized persons to unchurched communities to proclaim the Gospel in order to win converts to Jesus Christ, make disciples from the converts, and gather together the disciples to form functioning, multiplying local churches, that bear the fruit of the Kingdom of God in that community" – is to give them authority, freedom and power. In missions, churches and their leadership, through the person and leading of the Holy Spirit, take on this responsibility.

This has been the modus operandi throughout Church history. No doubt, the Church has had its ups and downs in empowering for missions. There are a variety of reasons for this, but the two main reasons are, the Church is not perfect and there is a spiritual enemy who infiltrates the Church to hinder the Church's leadership and their best intentions (1 Thess. 2.18). The enemy has been especially successful in hindering one key class of people to engage in missions and that is the poor. He has subtly done this by stigmatizing the poor as deplorable and useless. They are only to be pitied at best. The general mindset of the Church is, "Can anything good come out of our poor communities, slums and prisons." I give a resounding, YES, that God calls the poor and uses them to confound the wise and to expand and advance His Kingdom.

For close to four decades, I have been actively engaged in missions "from and for" the poor through the Christian missions organization, World Impact. The following thoughts are taken from World Impact's short article by Rev. Dr. Don Davis, *Our Distinctive: Advancing the Kingdom of God among the Urban Poor.* I have it in its entirety to stir the Church to see the poor as more than needing a hand-out.

God Has Chosen the Poor

One does not have to read many pages into the New Testament to discover where the early Church got the idea that the poor were specially chosen by God to receive the Gospel and spread it throughout the earth. Jesus, Himself, had announced publicly that He was intentionally preaching the Gospel to the poor (Luke 4.18, Luke 6.20) and even suggested that this action helped demonstrate that He was, indeed, the Messiah (Matt. 11.2-6).

Building on Jesus's teaching, it is not unusual to find very explicit statements in the Epistles about God's choice of, and expectations for, those who are without power, resources, or money. For example, James teaches: "Listen, my dear brothers: Has not God chosen those who are poor in the eyes of the world to be rich in faith and to inherit the kingdom he promised those who love him?" (James 2.5).

In a similar manner, Paul writes: "But God chose the foolish things of the world to shame the wise; God chose the weak things of the world to shame the strong; He chose the lowly things of this world and the despised things – and the things that are not – to nullify the things that are, so that no one may boast before Him" (1 Cor. 1.27-29).

The words "chose" and "chosen" in James 2 and 1 Corinthians 1 come from the Greek word *eklégomai* which means "giving favor to the chosen subject . . . It involves preference and selection from among many choices." In other contexts, it is used to describe God's choice of the "elect" (Mark 13.20) and Jesus's choosing of His disciples (Luke 6.13).

These ideas are not a new theme introduced by the New Testament writers. Instead, they faithfully reflect the Old Testament teachings about how God relates to the poor. One scholar summarizes the Old Testament teaching about the poor in three principles [Douglas J. Moo, *James, Tyndale Old Testament Commentary Series*, Gen. Ed. Leon Morris, (Leicester, England-Grand Rapids, MI: IVP-Eerdmans, 1985), pp. 53-54.]:

1. God has a particular concern for the poor.

2. God's people must have a similar concern [for the poor].

3. The poor are frequently identified with the pious and the righteous.

Who Are the Poor?

In the teaching of Jesus, material possessions are not regarded as evil, but as dangerous. The poor are often shown to be happier than the rich, because it is easier for them to have an attitude of dependence upon God.

~ R. E. Nixon. "Poverty." *The Illustrated Bible Dictionary.* Eds. J. D. Douglas, et al. Leicester, England: IVP, 1980. P. 1255

To understand God's choice of the poor it is necessary to understand who the "poor" are. The way that Scripture uses the term "poor" is both alike and different from the way we often use the term.

1. The Greek word used in the New Testament means essentially the same thing as our English word "poor." It describes someone who is economically deprived, someone who doesn't have enough money or resources. However, when this word is used by the New Testament writers, they seem to also rely on the Old Testament, the poor are both "those who don't have enough money" (Greek understanding) plus "something else" (Hebrew understanding).

2. This "something else" was an understanding developed over time in the Hebrew Scriptures. In the Old Testament, "the poor" are those who are so powerless and dependent that they are vulnerable to being misused by those who have influence in the society. The emphasis is on being on the wrong end of the relationship with those in power. Therefore, in the Old Testament, the poor came to mean those people who are characterized by three things:

   a. They lack the money and resources they need,

   b. They are taken advantage of by those who do have money and resources, and

   c. The result is that they must humbly turn to God as their only source of protection.

3. Therefore, from a theological point-of-view, we could say that the Scripture defines "the poor" as: "Those whose need makes them desperate enough to rely on God alone."

Biblical scholar Robert A. Guelich makes exactly these points when he writes about the development of the term "poor" in the Old Testament:

The most common of these words [for the poor], 'ny and its later relative, 'nw, have a much broader scope than simply to denote a socio-economic status. . . . The 'ny refers to one so powerless and dependent as to be vulnerable to exploitation by those who have the power base. Thus the accent falls on a socioeconomic relationship rather than on material possessions as such. Yet this powerless and dependent relationship caused one to rely upon God for one's needs and vindication. This humble posture of the

> poor devoid of pretension before God reflects the religious dimension and comes out frequently in the Psalms. . . . But the religious dimension is never exclusive of the socioeconomic. Both elements are integral to 'ny. . . . In summary, the poor in Judaism referred to those in desperate need (socio-economic element) whose helplessness drove them to a dependent relationship with God (religious element) for the supplying of their needs and their vindication.
>
> ~ Robert A. Guelich, The Sermon on the Mount. Waco: Word Books, 1982. pp. 68-69.

This understanding helps us perceive how Luke can record Jesus's teaching as "Blessed are the poor for yours is the Kingdom of God" (Luke 6:20); while Matthew records "Blessed are the poor in spirit for theirs is the Kingdom of heaven" (Matt. 5:3). In both accounts the point is the same: Blessed are those who become desperate enough to rely on God alone. Only people who are willing to acknowledge their helplessness can receive this help from God. As Clarence Jordan points out:

> When one says, "I don't need to be poor in things; I'm poor in spirit," and another says, "I don't need to be poor in spirit; I'm poor in things," both are justifying themselves as they are, and are saying in unison, "I don't need." With that cry on his lips, no man can repent.
>
> ~ Clarence Jordan, Sermon on the Mount, Rev. ed. Valley Forge: Koinonia Judson Press, 1980. p. 20.

Obviously, people who are not poor can come to this point of being desperate enough to rely on God alone. (The Bible records many examples, such as Zaccheus or Joseph of Arimathea, to make this apparent). It is also clear that many poor people may refuse to acknowledge their need before God. However, Jesus and the apostles consistently teach that it is even more difficult for the affluent to acknowledge their need for God (Matt. 19.24; Mark 10.23; James 2.6-7) and that the poor should be expected to respond with faith. This confidence in God's choice of the poor is so profound that one scholar can say: "In the New Testament the poor replace Israel as the focus of the gospel" (C. M. N. Sugden, "Poverty and Wealth," *New Dictionary of Theology*, eds. Sinclair B. Ferguson, et al., [Downers Grove: IVP, 1988], p. 524).

Four Fundamental Responses

To live in radical obedience to Jesus Christ means to be identified with the poor and oppressed. If that is not clear in the New Testament, then nothing is.

~ Jim Wallis, *Agenda for Biblical People.*
New York: Harper & Row, 1976. p.94.

When we recognize that the Scripture treats the poor as a group with theological significance, it forces us to consider what our response will be. Both as Christians, and as missionaries, there are at least four responses that we should make:

1. Respect

God's choice of the poor fundamentally challenges the normal way that people respond to the poor. Within society, people avoid the poor, disdain their ways, and expect little from them in any area. Certainly, they are not seen as the natural place to search for leaders.

God, however, identifies Himself with the poor. The Scriptures say that to oppress the poor is to show contempt to God Himself (Prov. 14.31). God's identification with the poor and

God's choice of the poor (James 2.5) should make a profound difference to anyone who acknowledges Christ as Lord. Simply put:

- If we respect God, we will respect the poor.

- If we obey God, we will identify with the poor.

- If we believe God, we will see the poor as the potential leaders of His Church.

Sadly, many people look at those who are poor and see them primarily as objects of benevolence. Such people view the poor only as those who need their help. While it is certainly right to help the poor (see point two below), such help will create dependence and a loss of dignity if it is not firmly coupled with deep respect for the poor as those that God has chosen. We believe it is not a sacrifice, but rather, a privilege and delight to be called to make disciples among the unreached urban poor.

2. Love, Compassion, and Justice

Christians are called to respond to others with love, compassion and justice. This response to the poor is the same response that Christians give to all people everywhere. What makes it unique is that the world system mitigates against applying this concern to the poor. Theologian Thomas C. Oden says:

> Although Christian charity is due everyone, the poor are Christ's particular concern, precisely because they are the neediest.
> ~ Thomas C. Oden, *Pastoral Theology: Essentials of Ministry.* San Francisco: Harper & Row, 1983. p.268.

God emphasizes our response to the poor, not to play favorites, but because otherwise they would be overlooked. The Scriptures constantly underscore the responsibility of God's people to share with the poor and help them escape from the grinding effects of poverty. God's Word places responsibility on us to work for justice for the poor. Working for shalom (peace, fullness, abundance, wholeness) means that we will never be content to leave the poor to their poverty while any of us have the means to affect change.

One of the ways that St. Francis described his relationship with the poor (and others) was through the word "cortesia." We use the word "courtesy" to mean manners. Originally, it meant the behavior and etiquette expected of one who served at a noble court.... For Francis ... *cortesia* was a way of seeing and acting towards others.

~ Lawrence Cunningham. *St. Francis of Assisi.*
San Francisco: Harper & Row, 1981.

3. Preach the Gospel

Out of all our responses to the poor, none is more important than preaching the Gospel. It is exactly what Jesus Himself did. Nothing is more revolutionary in liberating the poor than bringing them into relationship with God through Christ.

No project or program can ever achieve what salvation does for the poor. In coming to acknowledge Jesus as Lord and Savior, the poor experience radical liberation through the acquisition of an entirely new identity.

- They move from being at the bottom of the social structure to being an adopted child of the King of kings.

- God's favor, protection, and resources are made available through Christ.

- They are given authority over sin, hell, death, and every evil thing that would seek to destroy them.

- They are incorporated into a new community (the Church) which offers equality, respect, love, sharing, fellowship, and the opportunity to exercise their gifts and calling from God.

Salvation means that the presence of the living God is active among the poor bringing freedom, wholeness, and justice. It means that they are now part of a "royal priesthood," "members of a holy nation," in which they serve as "Christ's ambassadors" announcing hope and reconciliation to those around them who have not yet experienced liberation.

4. Expect Great Things

The intercession of a poor man is acceptable and influential with God.

~ The Pastor of Hermas. Bk. 3, *Ante-Nicene Fathers*, Vol. 2. Eds. A. Roberts and J. Donaldson, (Peabody, Hendrickson, 1995), p. 32.]

There is, perhaps, no more surprising statement that comes from Jesus's lips than the word He gives to His disciples in John 14.12-14:

I tell you the truth, anyone who has faith in me will do what I have been doing. He will do even greater things than these, because I am going to the Father. And I will do whatever you ask in my name, so that the Son may bring glory to the Father. You may ask for anything in my name, and I will do it.

On the surface, the idea of accomplishing greater things than Jesus seems absurd. And yet, in just a few short years the Book of Acts records more conversions than ever happen within the life and ministry of Jesus.

Two principles underlie this amazing statement. First, Jesus said discipleship reproduces students who are like Him (Luke 6.40). Second, when Jesus returned to the Father and sent the Holy Spirit (John 14.16; Acts 2.38), He made His power universally available to all who believe (John 14.14).

It would be easy to expect little from the poor because of their lack of resources. However, when Scripture disciplines our thinking, a new dynamic emerges. We expect congregations of the urban poor to do greater works than Jesus did on earth because they enter into a discipling relationship with Jesus who freely give them His Holy Spirit.

As we plant churches we must:

- Encourage the poor to believe in the calling, gifts, and abilities that God has given them, individually and corporately. We must have faith in what God will do through them even before they believe it themselves.

- Set high standards. The only acceptable goal for any Christian is to become like Jesus. Being poor is never an excuse for ignoring God's commands or shirking the responsibilities He gives every believer.

- Teach people to rely on Jesus, not on us. Missionary resources are limited. God's resources are unlimited.

- Instill a passion for reproduction (evangelism, follow-up, discipleship, and church planting). "You did not choose me, but I chose you to go and bear fruit – fruit will last.

Then the Father will give you whatever you ask in my name" (John 15.16).

One veteran missionary, who has served in both U.S. and Brazilian cities, describes successful churches among the urban poor in this manner:

> Churches . . . that used a "we-help-you-in-your-need" methodology were not winning the lower, working class. People were helped but the spiritual direction of their lives did not change . . . [whereas] churches that lacked financial and earthly resources were filled with poor people, were led by barely literate lay preachers, and made hard demands on people...The churches that gave the most and expected the least were not growing, but those that gave the least material benefit and demanded the most were growing fastest. They demanded conversion from sin and preached that Christ had the power to make it happen, and that this power could be received through faith and prayer.
>
> ~ Charles D. Uken,
> "Discipling White, Blue-Collar Workers and Their Families,"
> *Discipling the City: A Comprehensive Approach to the Urban Mission,*
> 2nd ed. Ed. Roger S. Greenway.
> Grand Rapids: Baker Book House, 1992. p. 180.

We honor both God and the poor when we respect them enough to believe that they will function as full-fledged disciples of Jesus Christ.

We believe there is a vast army of the poor, the prisoner, and the least-of-these who are the next wave of "authorized individuals" to expand and advance His Kingdom so that a healthy church is planted in every community of poverty around the world. These churches will be built upon a solid foundation, but their "framing and building" will look different. Many might even question if it is a "legitimate" church. Let the words of Watchman Nee speak to us:

> **Poor churches are not what they ought to be but they are more than what we think they are.**
>
> ~ Adapted from a letter from Watchman Nee to Norman Baker of CIM.
> *Reformation in Foreign Missions,* p. 49.
> Watchman Nee was a Chinese church leader and Christian
> teacher who worked in China during the 20th century.

The local church, no matter how small or poor, is the only place where the fruit of evangelism and discipleship is secured. They are an Outpost of the Kingdom of God and must be looked at in this way.

When Paul planted churches, they were considered churches from the very beginning. Though newly planted, these churches were biblical in the sense that they had all the rights, privileges, and responsibilities of a church. It is not a half church today and a full church tomorrow just as a baby born is not a half person. A baby is a full person but is expected to grow in strength and maturity. The church planted is fully a church. Paul would commend the small infant churches into God's hands, trusting the Holy Spirit to direct and empower the local appointed leaders to continue, at any cost, to grow and mature in the grace and knowledge of the Lord Jesus, and reproduce themselves. When Paul and his team arrived back in Antioch to give a report of their missions work they reported it as being fulfilled – "and from there they sailed to Antioch, where they had been commended to the grace of God for the work that they had fulfilled" (Acts 14.26). Paul knew when a disciple was made and when a church was established, for he reported his task as being completed/fulfilled.

The culmination of the Apostle Paul's missions' efforts was the establishment of a local church. "And when they had appointed elders for them in every church, with prayer and fasting they committed them to the Lord in whom they had believed" (Acts 14.23). Paul did not leave this to chance. The Apostle to the Gentiles was purposeful and strategic in making sure that the disciples gathered in a local assembly. Considering the centrality of the Church and the spiritual warfare we are engaged in, we must commit to establishing hundreds of thousands more "outposts of the Kingdom" in enemy occupied territory. An *Apostolic Missions Platform* commits to empowering by planting as many churches as we can as quickly as possible.

 **Connection:**
Rules of Engagement (ROE)

"Are you sure about this Lord?" "Your will be done and not mine." This is the tension of missions from beginning (the call) to the end (planted) and the entire process in between. Each step of the way, the church planter, must surrender all to the Holy Spirit (Apostolic Missions Plank) to effectively engage in the second "E" of our *Apostolic Missions Platform   Empowering.*

In 2001 HBO aired the war drama miniseries, *Band of Brothers.* It is based on the factual accounts of the 2nd Battalion, 506th Parachute Infantry Regiment of the 101st Airborne Division called "Easy Company." Over ten episodes, the series details the company's exploits during World War II. Lieutenant Colonel Ronald C. Speirs (20 April 1920–11 April 2007) was a United States Army officer who served in the 506th Parachute Infantry Regiment of the 101st Airborne Division during World War II.

In one particular scene, a Private named Albert Blithe, made a confession to Speirs:

Pvt. Blithe:	Lieutenant . . . sir, when I landed on D-Day, I found myself in a ditch all by myself. I fell asleep. I think it was, it was . . . airsickness pills they gave us. When I woke up, I didn't really . . . try to find my unit . . . to fight. I just . . . I just kinda stayed put.
Capt. Speirs:	What's your name, trooper?
Pvt. Blithe:	I'm Blithe, sir. Albert Blithe.
Capt. Speirs:	You know why you hid in that ditch, Blithe?
Pvt. Blithe:	I was scared.
Capt. Speirs:	We're all scared. You hid in that ditch because you think there's still hope. But Blithe, the only hope you have is to accept the fact that you're already dead. And the sooner you accept that, the sooner you'll be able to function as a soldier's supposed to function. Without mercy, without compassion, without remorse. All war depends upon it.

Not everything that Capt. Speirs said to Pvt. Blithe has a direct correlation to us as Kingdom people who are engaged in spiritual warfare. We are people of hope (1 Cor. 13.13), mercy (Luke 6.36), compassion (Eph. 4.32). There is an underlying principle though, from Speirs, that resonates to the core of life in Christ, and that is to "accept the fact that you're already dead." Paul the Apostle said the same truth to the community of believers in Colossae when he wrote, "If then you have been raised with Christ, seek the things that are above, where Christ is, seated at the right hand of God. Set your minds on things that are above, not on things that are on earth. For you have died, and your life is hidden with Christ in God. When Christ who is your life appears, then you also will appear with him in glory" (Col. 3.1-4). The sooner the church planter accepts the fact that they have been crucified with Christ and no longer live but Christ lives in them, the sooner they will be able to function as authorized representatives to advance and expand God's Kingdom into enemy occupied territory. All missions depend on it.

War automatically implies a conflict between powers. In missions, Satan's primary strategy, as mentioned above, is to kill the one who is authorized and sent to proclaim the gospel and establish and Outpost of the Kingdom of God in his territory. Day and night Satan makes his attacks and accusations before God Almighty (Rev. 12.10) against these representatives who herald good news of salvation and reconciliation in Jesus Christ. In fact, against all God's daughters and sons in the faith. How do we conquer these accusations? Revelation 12.11 gives us the answer, "And they have conquered him by the (1) blood of the Lamb and by (2) the word of their testimony, for they (3) loved not their lives even unto death."

When identifying and equipping called individuals to move forward in missions, these three qualities must be evident:

1. Blood of the Lamb. Is the cross alone for salvation solidified in the individual? It is not, "the blood of the Lamb" plus something else. They preach this Gospel to themselves daily in order to conquer the onslaughts of the lies and accusations of the Devil. The natural outflow is to proclaim this same blood of the Lamb, that allows them to conquer, to others, whether lost or saved. The blood of the Lamb is painted on the "door frames" of their life for all to see (Exod. 12.7).

2. The Word of their Testimony. This is a simple but powerful tool that must be clearly heard. Like the blind man's testimony, "Once I was blind but now I see" (John 9.25). Once I was lost, but now I'm found (Luke 15). Is there discernable evidence in the church planter's testimony, where like the blind man, they say, "One thing I do know . . ." A clear, compelling testimony rehearsed regularly in one's heart brings victory in the spiritual war.

3. Loved not their lives. There must be evidence in the individual who is called to missions that they are content in life (Phil. 4.11-13). Another way of saying it, "they have died, and their life is hidden in Christ." They already have some "wounds; scars" of sacrificial service for their Lord (2 Cor. 11.23-29). The words of Amy Carmichael fit the one who does not love their life, but have totally surrendered their life to the Lord:

Hast Thou No Scar?

Hast thou no scar?
No hidden scar on foot, or side, or hand?
I hear thee sung as mighty in the land;
I hear them hail thy bright, ascendant star.
Hast thou no scar?

Hast thou no wound?
Yet I was wounded by the archers; spent,
Leaned Me against a tree to die; and rent
By ravening beasts that compassed Me, I swooned.
Hast thou no wound?

No wound? No scar?
Yet, as the Master shall the servant be,
And piercèd are the feet that follow Me.
But thine are whole; can he have followed far
Who hast no wound or scar?

Another practical insight, and a word of encouragement, for church planters and those identifying (accessing) those who are called into missions, is the ability to teach sound, clear doctrine. There is a difference between preaching and teaching. My observation and experience have been that the Church's emphasis is on preaching. The more eloquent, creative, dynamic one is in preaching a sermon, the conclusion in many cases is, they are called to church planting. A dynamic preacher is good but what is better and needed is one who can teach and defend sound doctrine. Here's why:

1. When assessing an elder, one of the requirements is the ability to teach (2 Tim. 2.24; 1 Tim. 3.2). There is nothing wrong with wanting to be creative and eloquent in teaching, but teaching is about the communication of facts, i.e. sound doctrine. Titus 1.9 makes it very clear, "He must hold firm to the trustworthy word as taught, so that he may be able to give instruction in sound doctrine and also to rebuke those who contradict it."

2. The Apostle Paul himself was not eloquent in speech – "And I, when I came to you, brothers, did not come proclaiming to you the testimony of God with lofty speech or wisdom" (1 Cor. 2.1). In fact he was fearful and trembling when he came to speak in Corinth – "And I was with you in weakness and in fear and much trembling" (v. 3). Would the Apostle to the Gentiles, the planter of many churches, pass some of our church planting assessment centers due to his fear, trembling, and lack of lofty speech? Would he fit the unfortunate mold of what many are looking for in their planters and pastors? We must change our assessment from the pressure of preaching a 5-7 dynamic sermon at our church planting assessment centers to the assessing of our church planters' ability to teach in sound doctrine.

Are they able to defend our Sacred Roots, what the church has believed everywhere, always and by all?

3. The observation of a church planter's ability to teach is not primarily done at an assessment center through writing and responding to doctrinal questions. This critical requirement for missions must be observed and refined over time. There is no time frame given in Scripture. All we know is that it is required, and it must be observed over a period of time. Barnabas identified Paul the Apostle as one to engage in missions, so he went to Tarsus to bring him to the Church in Antioch (Acts 11.25-26a). For one year (Acts 11.26b) Paul is teaching. This allowed the elders to observe and assess Paul's teaching of sound doctrine and not just a onetime event. The Elders, in this case the assessors, through the timing and prompting of the Holy Spirit, gave the commission and release of the Apostle Paul to engage in missions (Acts 13.1-3).

One last practical insight for the commissioning and releasing of identified and equipped individuals for missions is the knowledge that they have already made disciples. This allows those who are assessing that the church planter has a plan of making a disciple from a convert. Heart and desire are not enough. There must be knowledge that has led to results, disciples made, before sending individuals into missions to evangelize, make disciples, that culminate in the planting of a church in Satan's domain. Make sure the church planter has made disciples – evangelism leading to conversion and then making a disciple of the convert. Remember, every church planter is a disciple maker but not every disciple maker is a church planter.

Connection Story

Joseph Biswas is an unassuming, gentle Bengali Spirit-filled follower of Jesus. Through this one humble, Spirit-filled person, we have been honored to equip, commission, and release several Bengali movement leaders, who in turn have equipped and released Bengali church planters leading to new Communities of the Kingdom being planted. Rejoice and be amazed at how the Holy Spirit empowers an unassuming Bengali follower to advance His Kingdom.

Pastor Joseph of the Evangelical Bengali Church in Queens had already started outreach in Jackson Heights but had a yearning for more. When he heard about World Impact's Evangel Schools of Urban Church Planting in 2017, it sounded like just what he needed to train more of his congregation to plant churches. Pastor Joseph arranged to meet with myself and Luke Raughley (World Impact staff). During this meeting Joseph arranged for one leader of the church, Oliver, to attend our Newark Evangel School of Urban Church Planting.

It did not take long to see the results. One week after Oliver returned, Pastor Joseph wanted to meet with us. "Oliver is a changed man," he said. "We need more of this." We began making plans on how to get Joseph and his Bengali team the resources and training they needed, and decided that the Evangel Dean Training that October in Wichita, Kansas, would enable Joseph to facilitate his own Evangel Schools in his context for his church plant teams.

Having no extra money to pay for the training and travel was a small hurdle to jump over. Another problem was that Oliver could not get paid leave from his job and he could not afford to lose the income since he needed it to support his family. He was so passionate about learning how to reach his community, that he was ready to quit his job to attend the training. I encouraged Oliver to trust the Lord and take unpaid leave from his job rather than quit. Through a partnership with Stadia, God provided.

We were able to compensate Oliver for his time away so that his family was provided for, and we covered the training and travel costs for the Evangel Dean Training.

In October, Pastor Joseph, Oliver, and other leaders from the Evangelical Bengali Church went to Wichita for the Evangel Dean School. (The Evangel Dean School is built on biblical principles and World Impact's fifty years of experience in urban ministry. We offer this training to equip churches, ministry networks, denominations, or movements to train church plant teams for their context. Evangel Dean Coaches walk with Dean Candidates through the Dean School and coach them for one year after the school as the Evangel Dean Team works toward hosting their first Evangel School of Urban Church Planting.)

Months later, in February 2018, another Evangel School of Urban Church Planting was hosted in Newark. Seven planters attended, and at the end of the school they were commissioned to go out and plant churches targeting the over 100,000 Bengali Muslims in the New York Metropolitan area. That March, Pastor Joseph returned to Bangladesh with a simplified "field manual" version of *Ripe for Harvest* (Our primary church planting manual) and hosted an Evangel School of Urban Church Planting for twenty-seven Christian leaders there.

Pastor Joseph's vision of a church planting movement in Bangladesh by no means slowed things back in America. In May, the Bengali Evangel Deans that had gone to Wichita hosted an Evangel School for their leaders. That August, two teams went to the same Evangel Dean Training school those leaders had attended last year. The first team, made up of four leaders, would go on to focus their church planting efforts in Bangladesh, and the second team would stay to reach the Bengali in the U. S. and Canada.

In 2019, I invited Pastor Joseph to the March Evangel Gathering in Wichita. (The Evangel Gathering is an annual convening event facilitated by the Evangel Network. The Evangel Network "dynamically catalyzes movements for health and multiplication.") Being with other church plant movement leaders greatly encouraged and inspired Joseph. It was here that he made plans for the Oklahoma Bengali leadership to attend the August Evangel Dean School.

That spring, Joseph traveled to Bangladesh again with fellow Evangel Deans from his congregation to facilitate church plant trainings. One training was held in South Bangladesh with about twenty-five local pastors. The other training was in North Bangladesh and was geared for church planters. Back in America, two more Bengali teams attended at yet another Evangel Dean School, one of whom was Alfred Biswas, from Oklahoma.

We were working hard to ensure the Bengali Christians had what they needed to spread the Gospel and plant more churches without financial strain. With the President of World Impact, Dr. Alvin Sanders, and myself, we secured a grant from the Finishing Fund to reach two "Unreached People Groups" in Bangladesh. Pastor Joseph was the connection to lead me to work with Samuel Bala, our contact person in Bangladesh.

The September of 2019, Alfred Biswas, now an Evangel Dean, sent me an email to give an update about his work in Bangladesh: "Greetings from Bangladesh! I am happy to inform you that we have planted another new church. This is fully MBB (Muslim Background Believers) church."

Just a few months after this update, the COVID-19 pandemic struck the world. Despite normal life coming crashing to a halt, Pastor Joseph's Bangladeshi church plant movement did not slow. Bony Baroi in Bangladesh, who had been trained at the 2018 Dean School, had a vision to baptize 30,000 new believers congregated in 1,000 new churches. Through much prayer and discussion, we settled on a plan that would enable him, by the power of the Holy Spirit, to accomplish this vision.

During this time I began consulting with Pastor Joseph to unite the Bengali Christian leaders he knows in nine states and Canada around evangelism, training, leadership, and church planting. This unity would lead to more conversions, leaders, and churches being planted, by the grace of God.

One of Pastor Joseph's connections, Prodip Das, attended the 2021 Evangel Dean School Training online. Within a couple of months of his commissioning, Prodip hosted an online Evangel School and was assisted by Rev. Dr. Baidya from New York and Rev. Halder from Bangladesh. At this school, eleven church planters and leaders were commissioned, representing six denominations and six different areas in Bangladesh. The leaders agree that more Evangel Schools need to be held to teach their people how to effectively reach more Bengalis. As part of their review process, they have planned to host an additional ten schools in the next two years. In one year, Prodip has facilitated four Evangel Schools of Urban Church planting. He is well on his way to reaching his goal of ten in two years.

Two pastors, Rev. Milon Sarker and Rev. Ashim Kumar, in Bangladesh heard about the training and contacted me about receiving training to be certified as Evangel Deans so they can host church planting trainings. Their connections in missions work and the Baptist denomination makes them excited to begin a church planting movement of their own. This may be yet another opportunity for another church planting movement that God is opening in Bangladesh.

Over the past four years, God has brought World Impact and the Christian Bengali community together to do great things. Not only did He give the pastors and leaders the passion for reaching their people, but He brought them to people who could help them harness that fire. Time and again our Bengali partners have shown that when they receive the tools and resources to succeed, they will.

One unassuming individual, submitted to the Lord Jesus and empowered by His Holy Spirit, is being used of God to see many Bengali people come to the obedient faith in Christ, be discipled, and established in a healthy church for the glory of God. Joseph is an inspiration and a reflection of one grounded in this apostolic missions plank – The Holy Spirit.

CHAPTER 3

THE GOSPEL: Evangelize

Key Old Testament Verse

And the king of Sodom said to Abram, "Give me the persons (Hebrew – souls) but take the goods for yourself."

~ Genesis 14.21

Key New Testament Verse

For I am not ashamed of the gospel, for it is the power of God for salvation to everyone who believes, to the Jew first and also to the Greek.

~ Romans 1.16

Contact: Situation Awareness

When I lived in South Central Los Angeles, Skid Row at one time was comprised of ten thousand homeless people in a six-to-eight block area. There were, and still are, tent and cardboard homes stretched out along the street like a row of condominiums in the suburbs. It is a community of poor, fractured, broken, hopeless people in need of hope in this world, and in the world to come, eternal life. I saw many people from all walks of life, filled with compassion, mercy, care, and kindness, enter this community of despair, to do ministry. Young and old, male and female, the rich and not so rich would serve at one of the shelters, or pass out food and clothes, give a listening ear, pray. I saw Christians and non-Christians alike in Skid Row who were actively and compassionately loving the least of these. One particular group especially stuck out in my regular Saturday trips into Skid Row. It was a Buddhist group.

Every week, fifty-one weeks out of the year, this Buddhist community would come to Spring Street and 7th, behind the Union Rescue Mission, to love and serve the poor, the addicts, the mentally ill who were living in the urine filled and violent streets of Skid Row. Their commitment to excellence and love would put many "Christians" to shame. They worked in harmony setting up their cooking grills and portable tents. I watched as they served hundreds of homeless people each Saturday. The food was served fresh, hot, and with love and kindness. The Buddhists would also pair up and look for those without shoes or shoes that were tattered and worn. Once they spotted someone they would kneel and wash their feet. They continued this act of kindness by putting new socks and shoes on the person. Their "niceness" was an excellent thing to behold. It was genuine compassion reaching out to those who were hurting, hopeless and homeless. It was right and it was good. It was humanity at its finest. What it wasn't though, was missions leading to eternal life.

 **Content 1:**
Missions Plank: *The Gospel*

Niceness – wholesome, integrated personality – is an excellent thing. We must try by every medical, educational, economic, and political means in our power, to produce a world where as many people as possible grow up 'nice'; just as we must try to produce a world where all have plenty to eat. But we must not suppose that even if we succeeded in making everyone nice we should have saved their souls. A world of nice people, content in their own niceness, looking no further, turned away from God, would be just as desperately in need of salvation as a miserable world – and might even be more difficult to save. . . . For mere improvement is no redemption, though redemption always improves people even here and now and will, in the end, improve them to a degree we cannot yet imagine. God became a man to turn creatures into sons: not simply to produce better men of the old kind but to produce a new kind of man.

~ C. S. Lewis, *Mere Christianity.*

C. S. Lewis clearly understood that niceness, though good, doesn't necessarily mean you're saved or lead to the salvation of souls. The Buddhists were nice people, but their niceness brought no eternal redemption of souls.

It was John Wesley who said, "You have one business on earth – to save souls; therefore, spend and be spent in this work." The Apostle Paul said the same thing to the Corinthian Church, "I will most gladly spend and be spent for your souls" (2 Cor. 12.15a). Why this focus on souls? Why has the Church throughout history, from Paul the Apostle to John Wesley to the Church of the twenty-first century, sacrificed everything, and in some cases their very lives, for those lost without Christ?

The crowning of all God's creation is man and woman, for they are created in the image of God (Gen. 1.27; Ps. 8). When God breathed His life into man, he became a living soul (Gen. 2.7); an eternal being. Souls are not distinguished by ethnicity, color, race, gender, age, or class. God looks past the outer distinctions of His creation – "I praise you, for I am fearfully and wonderfully made" (Ps. 139.14) – and looks at the inward eternal soul of a person. The Scriptures are clear that the soul does not die when the body dies (Eccles. 12.5-7; Matt. 17.1-3; 22.31-32; Luke 16.19-31; 23.39-43; Rev. 6.9). Not only is this scriptural but the early church fathers found this to be so important as a doctrine that it was included in our sacred roots. The Nicene Creed states, "We look to the resurrection of the dead, and the life of the world to come. Amen."

Though the body of every human will return to dust upon death, the soul survives eternally, either to a life of eternal fellowship with God or to a life of eternal separation from God; either eternity in heaven or eternity in hell; either a life of eternal bliss and shalom or a life of eternal woe and torment. The tragic news is that every soul, from Adam and Eve to now and into the future, was and is born into the bondage of sin and are at enmity with God (Gen. 6.5; Ps. 51.5; Eccles. 7.20; Rom. 3.23, 5.12; Eph. 2.3). The destiny of the souls of all humankind is automatically determined to be separated from God and His presence. There is no escape. All are doomed. We are helpless and hopeless on the road to eternal destruction (Matt. 7.13-14). The criticalness of sin not only leads to the eternal reality of hell, but it will lead to such chaos on the earth that if God "does not cut the days short," we would destroy each other (Mark 13).

Though we do not like to hear it, God is at war with us. We are all rebels and have rebelled against our Creator, God Almighty, and He must deal with the rebellion (2 Pet. 2.4-10). These are high stakes. The wrong decision has catastrophic eternal consequences. The eternity of hell is far worse than the temporal deepest needs and poverty of humanity. It is separation and torment from God that will have no end. The Scriptures are clear:

> And many of those who sleep in the dust of the earth shall awake, some to everlasting life, and some to shame and everlasting contempt.
>
> ~ Daniel 12.2

> And these will go away into eternal punishment, but the righteous into eternal life.
>
> ~ Matthew 25.46

And if your eye causes you to sin, tear it out. It is better for
you to enter the kingdom of God with one eye than with two
eyes to be thrown into hell, "where their worm does not die,
and the fire is not quenched."

~ Mark 9.47-48

... in flaming fire, inflicting vengeance on those who do
not know God and on those who do not obey the gospel of
our Lord Jesus. They will suffer the punishment of eternal
destruction, away from the presence of the Lord and from the
glory of his might.

~ 1 Thessalonians 1.8-9

And the smoke of their torment goes up forever and ever, and
they have no rest, day or night, these worshipers of the beast
and its image, and whoever receives the mark of its name.

~ Revelation 14.11

The battle between God and Satan is ultimately for souls. Souls
are the currency of the universe. Souls from every nation, people,
tribe, and language. From God's perspective the family lineage
that matters most is the spiritual one. According to John the Apostle,
every individual is either a child of the devil or a child of God,
"By this it is evident who are the children of God, and who are the
children of the devil: whoever does not practice righteousness is
not of God, nor is the one who does not love his brother" (1 John
3.10). God is claiming back souls bound in the domain of Satan
and adopting them into His family line to be His daughters and
sons, and the power that God uses, the only power to rescue,
claim, redeem, reconcile, restore, and adopt, is the Gospel of Jesus
Christ His Son. It is God's way, His truth, and His life (John
14.6). Jesus is the demonstration of God's love (John 3.16; Rom.
5.8). There is no other way to be saved except in name of Jesus
(Acts 4.12). There is no Plan B; no back up.

The fact of the matter is that we can't do this. We are bankrupt and powerless. Self-redemption is an utter impossibility. It is the core purpose for Jesus's Sermon on the Mount. Jesus not only upheld the moral and religious ideas and consciousness but took it to the next level when He declared, "You have heard it said . . . but I say to you." He needed to bring bankruptcy, hopelessness, despair, utter impossibility of self-redemption, self-rescue, in order that we would cry out to God for help . . . for salvation. "This is the end of self-redemption. Here is the very heart of Jesus's ethical teaching: the renunciation of self-attained righteousness and the willingness to become like children who have nothing and must receive everything" (*A Theology of the New Testament*, George Eldon Ladd). Jesus went on to say, "For what will it profit a man if he gains the whole world and forfeits his soul? Or what shall a man give in return for his soul?" (Matt. 16.26).

Only the Gospel of Jesus Christ has the power to break through the temporal into the eternal and transform one who is spiritually dead into one who is alive, adopted, and eternally secured in the roll call of heaven. Because of this, the Church's priority, its focused attention, must be on souls and the Gospel. If the Gospel of Jesus Christ is the only power to rescue from hell and the bondage of sin and Satan's kingdom, then we better have a clear understanding of what is the Gospel? Not a half Gospel but a complete, full Gospel. This has been the cunning deception of Satan since the Garden of Eden. He spoke a half-truth, which is a whole lie, leading Eve to question the God of all Truth. "Did God actually say . . .?" This half-truth led to the fall and rebellion of humanity. So, what is the full Gospel?

Literally the Gospel is the revelation of God's love, in Jesus Christ, for all humanity past, present and future (John 3.16; Heb. 1.1-4). It is derived from the Anglo-Saxon term god-spell, meaning the "good story" or in the Greek rendering evangelion, "good news." What is this good story, this good news, that is so powerful that can change the eternal address of a soul and transport them from the Kingdom of Darkness to the Kingdom of God?

Every story is comprised of key elements. These elements, when put together communicate the full story. There are a variety of excellent tools and models that communicate the full Gospel story. Here is a simple tool that I have designed called the five "Ps" of The Gospel. It is easy to memorize. Each "P" (element) of the Gospel has a corresponding short phrase that introduces the "P". All five elements are necessary to share in one way or another for the whole Gospel message to be fully declared. There is no limit to one's imagination on building upon each element. This allows for any culture to expand on the "P" (element) with their stories, history, values, beliefs, attitudes, behaviors, without compromising the critical elements of the Gospel. The five "Ps" of the Gospel are described as follows along with key verses:

1. Purpose: The Reign of God

Every kingdom has boundaries which the king has rule and reign over. Within those boundaries are the subjects of the rule of that king. When God created the world, and all that is in it, His creative work was good, perfect, and He reigned over it in love, for God is love (1 John 4.8b). His crowning work was Adam and Eve, the first man and woman, for they were created in His very image. They had perfect fellowship and relationship with their Creator. A relationship of love, honor, and respect. (Gen. 1; Ps. 19.1-4; Phil. 2.9-11; Rev. 11.15). God's Kingdom, His rule and reign, extended to all His creation. Adam and Eve were at perfect peace, resting in God's perfect rule and reign.

2. Problem: The Wrath of God

Adam and Eve were not content to rest in the peace of God's perfect rule and reign in their lives. Through the deception of a fallen created angel, Satan (the ancient Serpent) deceived them and led them into rebellion against their Creator (Gen. 3.1-7). They sought to be the ruler of their own domain and lives. This rebellion against the rightful Ruler and Creator of all things has incurred His wrath and He is justified to judge, condemn, and mete out punishment to the rebels and their rebellion (Gen. 3.8-19). The verdict is guilty on all charges and the punishment was quick, severe (pain and death), and leading to banishment from the righteousness, joy and peace of His rule and reign (Gen. 3.22-24).

Everyone must be confronted with the terrible truth of sin and the wrath of God upon sin. (Rom. 1.18; 2.5; 3.23; 6.23; Gen. 3.21-24; Rom. 3.10-18; 2 Thess. 1.7-9; Rev. 19.15b). All of humanity is infected and bound in sin (Romans 3.23) making us enemies of God (Romans 5.10). This is a crisis of incalculable magnitude as the wrath of God could be poured out at any moment (Rom. 1.18; 2.5; Rev. 14.9-11; John 3.36; Jon. 3.7-9). Sin is a cancerous infection that has ravaged the entire human race and threatens its very existence.

> The plight of man in his fallen condition is pathetic. His maimed, paralyzed, blighted, darkened, blinded, enslaved, fearing, dreading, hating, fleeing, scheming, and plotting condition and attitude make man the most miserable and the most dangerous of all creatures. . . . Sin is moral perversity, social evil, a false direction of mind, affection, relationship and life. . . . Sin is man confronting God in rational (or irrational) disbelief, in volitional disobedience, in brazen self-love, self-rule, self-redemption, self-worship. . . . One sin is incipient war with God and all good, a league with the devil and all evil, a potential hell replacing heaven. It is not merely assault upon the throne of God; it is the blow struck full at the face of the Father.
>
> ~ George Eldon Ladd, *A Theology of the New Testament.*

Sin cannot be overstated. God's wrath is justified.

3. Plan: The Love of God

God has not destined the rebels for wrath (1 Thess. 5.9). God's boundless and overflowing love caused Him to devise a plan to rescue and save all of humanity from His judgement, condemnation, and punishment (John 3.16-17). His desire, flowing out of His matchless love, is that none should perish but that everyone would be saved and receive His peace rather than experience His enmity and just wrath (2 Pet. 3.9). This is the heart of the "Good News" – God has taken the initiative to seek and to save (Luke 19.10) those who have rebelled against His Kingdom, i.e., His rule and reign. Here is the love of God, not that we have loved God but that he loved us and sent his Son, whose name is Jesus, to be the propitiation for our sins (1 John 4.10). This Son of His appeased His wrath that is upon us (Rom. 3.24-25). We no longer need to be His enemies (Col. 1.21-22; Rom. 5.10-11). But how did Jesus, the Son of God, appease God's wrath so that we are no longer enemies of God? What did He do?

Jesus took our judgement, condemnation, and punishment upon Himself by being a sacrifice to God (John 1.29; Rom. 5.6-10; Eph. 5.2; Heb. 10.10). It was a brutal sacrifice of death upon a Roman cross. Jesus could be that sacrifice for the whole world because He was without sin and rebellion against God. He was perfect. 2 Corinthians 5.21 says, "For our sake he [God] made him [Jesus] to be sin who knew no sin, so that in him [Jesus] we might become the righteousness of God."

The Good News is that God actually saves us from Himself (Luke 2.14; 2 Cor. 5.21; Rom. 3.21-26; 5.1, 8-11; 1 Thess. 1.10; Col. 1.20; Isa. 53.5; 61.10; Eph. 2.14-18; Heb. 8.12). When Jesus cried out on the cross, "It is finished," He was stating that the war and wrath of God towards His rebellious enemies, humanity, has ended.

"For God so loved the world, that he gave his only Son, that whoever believes in him should not perish but have eternal life. For God did not send his Son into the world to condemn the world, but in order that the world might be saved through him." Those who believe in this plan of God's love through His Son, the Lord Jesus, are:

A. Saved from God's wrath (Rom. 5.9)

B. Granted peace with God (Rom. 5.1). We can have peace with God because God is now at peace with us; his wrath is removed.

C. Reconciled to God without our sins being counted against us (Rom. 5.10-11; 2 Cor. 5.19). "Blessed are those whose lawless deeds are forgiven, and whose sins are covered; blessed is the man against whom the Lord will not count his sin" (Rom. 4.7-8).

D. Declared children of His through adoption (Eph. 1.5).

E. Now declared righteous before God (Phil. 3.9). The biblical idea is not that God makes the sinner righteous but that He declares the sinner to be righteous. This is the root concept of justification, that those who respond to God's love in Christ through obedient faith, sinful though they may be, are declared righteous (Rom. 5.9). They are viewed as being righteous because in Christ Jesus they have been reconciled to God and are now in a righteous relationship with God the Father. Righteousness in this way centers on the demands laid upon the individual by God. That demand is to submit to the love of God by faith in Christ Jesus and to not seek self-redemption. "For, being ignorant of the righteousness of God, and seeking to establish their own, they did not submit to God's righteousness. For Christ is the end of the law for righteousness to everyone who believes" (Rom. 10.3-4). We are covered with the robe of

God's righteousness, "I will greatly rejoice in the Lord; my soul shall exult in my God, for he has clothed me with the garments of salvation, he has covered me with the robe of righteousness" (Isa. 61. 10a).

God's love is seeking out the rebels and inviting them to submit themselves to his reign that he might be their Father and their God. A peace treaty, through Jesus Christ, has been placed on the table of our hearts ready for any-and-all to be signed. This is good news, but it's all contingent upon the next "P" – *The Command of God.*

4. Priority: The Command of God

The nature of Christian missions is one of emergency. It's not about tomorrow but about today (2 Cor. 6.1-2). In this conflict of kingdoms there are sides. Everyone must decide and join a side. This is the priority. This is the command of God. Everyone is to decide what to do with God's loving invitation in Jesus Christ. Choose you this day which side you're on (Josh. 24.14-15; Exod. 32.26). Jesus is the only way to peace with God the Father; He is the one and only truth leading to reconciliation with God the Father; He is the only one to bring life, life abundantly and eternal, with God the Father – "Jesus said to him, 'I am the way, and the truth, and the life. No one comes to the Father except through me'" (John 14.6). Those who believe in God's plan of salvation and turn (repent) in obedient faith in the Lord Jesus will be saved (Mark 1.14-15; Rom. 10.9-10; 1 John 1.9; Acts 2.38; 3.19; 2 Cor. 7.9-10; John 6.40). Those who do not believe, remain sinners in the hands of an angry God.

God's love has been demonstrated to us that while we were still sinners, rebels, enemies of the God's kingdom rule and reign, Jesus willingly came to this enemy occupied world of corruption and bondage, and, died upon a cross to take God's wrath upon Himself rather having God's wrath rightfully dispensed upon us

(Rom. 5.8; Matt. 27.46; 2 Cor. 4.4). Oh, how great a love the Father has given us. God's command and our priority is to flee from the wrath that is to come (Matt. 3.7). It is inevitable. One can run from it for a while, but one cannot hide from it. "The time is fulfilled, and the kingdom of God is at hand; repent and believe in the gospel" (Mark 1.15).

5. Proof: The Expectation of God

The expectation of God is that we work out this salvation decision in fear and trembling knowing that He is at the same time working in us His good pleasure to conform us into the image of His Son in whom He loves (Phil. 2.12-13 w/Rom. 8.29). What is our part in working this out?

A. *Belief.* After Jesus fed the 5,000, the crowd got into boats and went to Capernaum where Jesus and his disciples had gathered. They were seeking Jesus for more bread. He was like a walking bakery to the people. Jesus, knowing their hearts, challenged them to work for food that endures to eternal life which Jesus was willing to give them (John 6.27). In response they asked a logical question to Jesus's challenge to work, "What must we do, to be doing the works of God?" (John 6.28). That's a fair-enough question. Jesus responds with God's expectation, "This is the work of God, that you believe in him whom he has sent." Believing is to work out our salvation. The enemy, the world, and our own sinful passions and desires to rule our lives, demand a constant work on our part to believe that Jesus is God's one plan for salvation. The demonic forces of the Satanic kingdom will constantly tempt you, like Jesus was tempted, but twisted differently. Instead of, "If you are the Son of God" (Matt. 4.3, 6), he tempts us with, "Is He really the Son of God; the Way, the Truth, and The Life?" This is hard work that requires endurance and discipline. It is to take every thought, half-truth and full lie, captive to the obedience of Christ (2 Cor. 10.5). It takes daily work, struggle, effort, to "not throw away your confidence" (Heb. 10.35). It takes death to one's very self.

B. *Self-Death*. Self-death can seem morbid, sick, gloomy, downright unrealistic and "too" spiritual. It's for monks and radical lunatics. Yet, the Lord calls those to discipleship to make an unqualified decision so radical that it involves turning his or her back upon all other relationships (Luke 9.58-61; Matt. 10.34-39). All personal goals and ambitions must be brought to the Lord and put to death (Gal. 2.20). The decision to be made is one in which all self-rule is relinquished, sacrificed, slain, and is replaced with a desire only for the rule and reign of God to have its rightful place in one's life (Luke 9.23). This makes perfect sense when seen through our status as priests. Peter the Apostle declared this high and holy status when he wrote, "you yourselves like living stones are being built up as a spiritual house, to be a holy priesthood, to offer spiritual sacrifices acceptable to God through Jesus Christ (1 Pet. 2.9). Priests were set apart and had responsibilities (Exod. 28.1; 1 Chron. 23.13). They had no inheritance except the Lord Himself (Deut. 10.9; 18.2). They belonged solely to the Lord. They were His and He was theirs. Self-death isn't for monks and radical lunatics but for the priesthood of all believers. Don't let the enemy deceive you into a soft, therapeutic Christianity. It is not about what you receive but about what you can give. In the kingdom economy, self-death is abundant life, "I have been crucified with Christ. It is no longer I who live, but Christ who lives in me. And the life I now live in the flesh I live by faith in the Son of God, who loved me and gave himself for me" (Gal. 2.20). Jesus came to give life and an abundant life (John 10.10). It's praying, "Your Kingdom come, and your will be done." It's declaring daily that you have been made a kingdom and priests to our God and shall reign on the earth for eternity (Rev. 5.10).

It is impossible for anyone who has made this radical decision of obedient faith and to be reconciled to God and adopted as His child, to not show and demonstrate the reality of this new transformation as a new creation in Christ (2 Cor. 5.17) and transference from the dark prince and his kingdom to the Lord Jesus and the Kingdom of God (Col. 1.13). God begins His work of sanctification through the person of the Holy Spirit and will bring it to completion on the eschatological day when Jesus will present the redeemed, perfected in holiness, unto God (Phil. 1.6).

The expectation of God is that the rule and reign of His Kingdom be reflected in His adopted children. They are to bear fruit (Matt. 3.8) and perform the deeds (Acts 26.20) that reflect a turning from one direction in life to the direction that points towards the Kingdom of God. This character of Jesus must be recognized by all (Matt. 7.20) through the fruit of the Holy Spirit (Gal. 5.22-23) in their life. We are to keep in step with the Holy Spirit (Gal. 5.25) and to walk as Jesus walked (1 John 2.6). It is expected that we, "put on the Lord Jesus Christ, and make no provision for the flesh, to gratify its desires" (Rom. 13.14). There should be proof of one's love for the Family of God (2 Cor. 8.24; Col. 3.12-14).

This is the Good News revealed in Christ to all of humanity. Jesus's cry to all is still the same, "Come to me, all who labor and are heavy laden, and I will give you rest. Take my yoke upon you, and learn from me, for I am gentle and lowly in heart, and you will find rest for your souls. For my yoke is easy, and my burden is light" (Matt. 11.28-30). He now has called the priests of His Kingdom to be the blessed feet that will bring this incredibly good news to the world, beginning right where we are (Rom. 10.15).

Content 2:
"E" of an Apostolic Missions Platform:
Evangelism

The International Buddhist Relief Organization is a UK-based NGO recognized by the UN. It was established as a charity in 1995 with the registered aim "to help relieve the suffering of people everywhere, regardless of their status, creed, or geographical location, who are in condition of need, hardship, or distress as a result of local, national, or international disaster or by reason of social or economic circumstances. In accordance with the Buddhist doctrine and principles, such help is also extended to animals everywhere that are in need of care or attention."

The mission of the Islamic Relief USA is "to provide relief and development in a dignified manner regardless of gender, race, or religion, and works to empower individuals in their communities and give them a voice in the world." They have a vision to, "work together for a world free of poverty." Their actions in tackling poverty are "marked by excellence in our operations and conduct, which are deserving of the people we serve." In responding to poverty and suffering, "our efforts are driven by sincerity to God and the need to fulfill our obligations to humanity." And their work is "founded on enabling people and institutions to fulfill the rights of the poor and vulnerable. We work to empower the dispossessed toward realizing their God-given human potential and developing their capabilities and resources."

Then there is the social services and disaster relief branch of the Islamic Circle of North America, ICNA Relief. During COVID-19, the writing of this booklet (ICNA Relief website), they have distributed 239,204 food boxes; 104,609 hot meals; 9,568,160 pounds of food and groceries; served 357,841 children; 183,154 families; 731,473 individuals; 51,026 elderly; 11,636 hygiene kits distributed; had 7,779 volunteers. The value of the food boxes alone was $11,960,200 in which 382 cities were served.

If I didn't inform you that these groups were either Buddhist or Islamic you could easily have mistaken them as a Christian organization or a local church serving the poor or those who encounter an unforeseen disaster. Yes, they are to be commended for their service, compassion, giving and care to those in need. This is what humanity, regardless of religion, does, knowing that crisis, pain, sorrow, hits us all whether we are saved or not, no matter what language we speak, where we live, what our faith is. To meet needs and address injustices is what God expects from all of humanity. But this isn't Christian missions.

> It is a mischievous doctrine to think that missions must aim at the total reorganization of the whole social value. From the experience of the church, from the example of our Lord and His apostles they did not aim directly at such an end. They were content at implanting the life of Christ in the hearts of men and were willing to leave the consequences to the care of God.
>
> ~ G. W. Peters

Christopher Little captured this sentiment in a 2008 article he wrote for the *International Journal of Frontier Missions* 25, no. 2: 68 (See also in the same issue, "Responses to Christopher Little's 'What Makes Mission Christian?'" 75-78). "There is nothing particularly Christian about humanitarian work in the first place. For example, Bill Gates, Oprah Winfrey, the United Nations, USAID, Oxfam, the Red Cross and Red Crescent, etc., are all striving to alleviate the ailments of humanity for basically philanthropic reasons."

Demonstrations of mercy, justice and compassion are demonstrations of humanity's mandate from God whether they recognize God or not. Those who are followers of

Jesus and those who are not, participate to alleviate the brokenness, hurt, pain and injustices of the world we live in. God has given to all humanity the responsibility and requirement to do justly, love mercy and walk humble with God (Mic. 6.8). The Hebrew definition for "man" in Micah 6.8 is – mankind (male and female), anyone, any man, men, mortal, people, population, humanity. This is a human race mandate and all men and women, whether children of God or not are to do justly, love mercy and walk humbly with their God. In humanity's best moments, they have still fallen short in each of these areas – justice, mercy, walking with God. Jesus, as the perfect Man, the Son of Man, the complete representation of humanity as they were created to be before the Fall, demonstrated these three requirements of God, to perfection. His life was the perfect reflection of humanity, of what it looks like to do justly, love mercy and walk humbly with God.

Acts of compassion and justice are not the power of God that can bring salvation. Neither are miracles a guarantee that people will respond in faith to God's plan of salvation in Jesus Christ. Jesus did the miraculous as a demonstration of the power of the Kingdom of God invading the territory of the "prince of the power of the air" (Eph. 2.2). During His ministry, Jesus performed more than forty miracles (an event that is outside the bounds of natural law) including healing the sick, changing the natural elements of nature and even raising people from the dead. Jesus performed miracles to minister, glorify the Father, to reveal Himself as being sent by God (approved Acts 2.22), and to give us a foretaste of the Kingdom to come but they necessarily didn't lead to repentance and salvation.

Raising Lazarus from the dead didn't change the heart of many towards Jesus as the Messiah (John 11.45-53). Only one out of ten lepers who were miraculously cleansed and healed returned in faith to express gratitude to Jesus. "Your faith has saved you," was Jesus's reply (Luke 17.14-19). His "salvation" or wholeness was more than physical healing. It implied a sound spiritual state. Feeding five thousand miraculously (John 6) wasn't enough of a demonstration to lead most to faith in Jesus. In fact, only twelve remained of the five thousand. They looked at Jesus and said, "You have the words of eternal life, and we have believed, and have come to know, that you are the Holy One of God."

In Jesus's story of the Rich Man and Lazarus (Luke 16.19-31) we read that the way to repentance is the proclamation of Jesus and upon hearing the good news to then repent and believe. We know the story. A nameless rich man and a poor man named Lazarus both die. Lazarus is, "carried by the angels to Abraham's side" while the rich man is, "in anguish in this flame," and is separated from Abraham and Lazarus by a great chasm. The rich man begs Abraham to send Lazarus from the dead to warn his five brothers of this eternal torment and separation from God but Abraham replies, "They have Moses and the Prophets; let them *hear* them." But the rich man doesn't think that's enough and in reply says, "No, Father Abraham, but if someone goes to them from the dead, they will repent." He was convinced they needed a visible demonstration of the greatest of miracles – someone coming back to life from the grave. This would turn them towards repentance and salvation. Abraham again states in these last words to the rich man, "If they do not *hear* Moses and the Prophets, neither will they be convinced if someone should rise from the dead." Who is the fulfillment of the Law (given to Moses) and Prophets? Jesus is the fulfillment (Matt. 5.17; Rom. 8.3-4). The only way towards repentance and salvation is to hear the good news of Jesus.

The goal of missions is not the transformation of culture. Transformation of culture is a by-product of missions. When the spiritually dead respond to the obedient faith in Jesus Christ, that life is transformed into a new creation and transferred into a new culture, a kingdom culture. John Piper said it right, "The way to achieve the greatest social and cultural transformation is not to focus on social and cultural transformation, but on the "conversion" of individuals . . . to faith in Jesus Christ for the forgiveness of sins and the hope of eternal life" (*Missions: Rescuing from Hell and Renewing the World*). The goal and task of missions is to win converts to the rule and reign of God's Kingdom through allegiance to the King of God's Kingdom. It all begins with the feet of those who bring Good News (Rom. 10.14-15). What the world needs, what the criticalness of the times demand, is proclamation of the power of God that brings salvation to everyone who believes (Rom. 1.16). The world needs to hear in order to have the opportunity to believe.

Jesus set a clear pattern on how the Gospel was going to spread when He said to His disciples, "I must preach the good news of the kingdom of God to the other towns as well; for I was sent for this purpose" (Luke 4.43). Jesus and His Apostles clearly place a priority of evangelism above compassion and justice. If anyone is to come to salvation in Christ Jesus, they must hear and receive a clear presentation of the Gospel. Doing a quick read through the book of Acts, one will read that the Apostle Paul did not do one demonstration of justice or compassion (except the miraculous exorcism of the slave girl which was a power encounter) yet disciples were made, and churches were planted throughout the Roman provinces. How? The Apostle to the Gentiles proclaimed the Gospel.

The lost come to the obedient faith by confessing Jesus Christ as Lord through the proclamation of the Gospel. Rom. 10.14-17 states is simply, "How then will they call on him in whom they have not believed? And how are they to believe in him of whom they have never heard? And how are they to hear without someone preaching? And how are they to preach unless they are sent? As it is written, 'How beautiful are the feet of those who preach the good news!' But they have not all obeyed the gospel. For Isaiah says, 'Lord, who has believed what he has heard from us?' So, faith comes from hearing, and hearing through the word of Christ."

It is all about the message and not the messenger. The message alone, through the working of the Holy Spirit, "convicts the world of sin, righteousness, and judgment" (John 16.8). Messengers are just a vessel in which the message of the Gospel is spoken. The early Church was not persecuted because of demonstrations of compassion and justice but because of their confession and proclamation that Jesus is the risen Lord and is to be worshipped and glorified alone. All of humanity can and must do acts of kindness, compassion, justice, and mercy but only the Church, the priesthood of all believers, can and must proclaim the Gospel. For the one who is authorized and sent to plant churches, this becomes their first task. It is their priority and responsibility. No church will be planted apart from the conversion of the lost and the lost cannot be converted unless they hear the Good News of Jesus Christ.

More than 100 times Jesus's ministry is described in terms of teaching, preaching, and evangelizing. More than 140 times the New Testament uses such words as "to announce", "to tell thoroughly", to "spread good news"; to herald or proclaim. Evangelism is critical to our *Apostolic Missions Platform* (Acts 4.4; 13.47-48; 16.25-34; 17.10-12; 17.32-34; 28.24; Eph. 1.13; Rom. 10.14). Paul the Apostle, the church planter to the Gentiles, ordered his missions calling and priority in the preaching of the Gospel (1 Cor. 15.1-5). G.W. Peters said, "Evangelization refers to the initial phase of Christian Ministry. It is the authoritative proclamation of the gospel of Jesus Christ as revealed in the Bible in relevant and intelligible terms, in a persuasive manner with the definite purpose of making Christian converts. It is preaching the gospel of Jesus Christ for a verdict." He goes on to state, "We are sent not to preach sociology but salvation; not economics but evangelism; not reform but redemption; not culture but conversion; not progress but pardon; not a new social order but a new birth; not revolution but regeneration; not renovation but revival; not resuscitation but resurrection; not a new organization but a new creation; not democracy but the gospel; not civilization but Christ; we are ambassadors not diplomats."

The most beautiful and relevant presentation of God's relation to the nations, the outcast, vile, evil, is found in the book of Jonah. Nineveh is completely outside the bounds. Nahum 3.1 describes this city as, "the bloody city, all full of lies and robbery." It was a center for the worship of Ishtar (Astarte) the fertility goddess. The military rulers were, "a brutal breed." They ruled their empire and subdued nations with absolute terror and yet God's desire, flowing out of His heart of love, compassion and mercy, was that the Ninevites would repent. God calls and sends Jonah not to set up a compassion ministry or to deal with the injustices that were taking place in Nineveh. God calls and sends Jonah to proclaim a message of repentance and turning from idolatry to the one true Creator God. The word that Jonah brought, without any demonstration of compassion, justice or even miracles, turned a Kings heart to cry out for forgiveness and to lead the entire city in repentance.

Think also of the cultural challenges in Paul's day. Slavery was an abusive and degrading institution; infanticide, the killing of unwanted babies, was common throughout the Roman Empire; the thirst for blood, violence and gluttony is captured by the people's cry, "give us bread and games"; temple prostitution was normal practice in the context of religious worship; women in Ancient Rome did not have equal legal status with men; prostitution in ancient Rome was legal and licensed. Not to mention the brutality and swiftness to maintain the peace, the corruptions and injustices of politics, police force (no body cams); political corruption. And then there was the inescapable health issues of the Roman Empire. "Infectious disease was long part of Roman life. Even the richest Romans could not escape the terrors of a world without germ theory, refrigeration, or clean water. Malaria and intestinal diseases were, of course, rampant" (*Smithsonian Magazine*, April 2020).

In all the cultural ills of Paul's time, his focus wasn't on transforming the culture through addressing the evils and life struggles confronting him. His focus was evangelism. "For I decided to know nothing among you except Jesus Christ and him crucified" (2 Cor. 2.2).

> The Church of Christ in all its complex service to the world can never forget that its primary concern is to call man into and prepare them for the life eternal . . . it is obvious that from the Christian standpoint no greater injury can be done to the true progress and healing of humanity in this present evil world than to make it promises and offer it remedies which have no vital connection with the hope of eternal life.
>
> ~ Geerhardus Vos, *The Eschatology of the Psalms*, pp. 363-364.

I love the way A. W. Tozer said it, "Jesus didn't come to save us from our problems. He came to save us from our sin." People are eternal. There is no other way to be saved. There is a hell. There is only one hope for this world and that is the Gospel. Christian missions and the Gospel have one focus and that focus is souls . . . the currency of the universe. It is the only power (Rom. 1.16) that can exchange the currency of souls from the hands of Satan into the hands of God – "He has delivered us from the domain of darkness and transferred us to the kingdom of his beloved Son, in whom we have redemption, the forgiveness of sins" (Col. 1.13-14). We have been given stewardship of this power and this stewardship centers on proclamation.

> Here is the sacred and tremendous responsibility of the church toward the world. If the church fails to preach God's way of forgiveness of sins, no one else will and the world will remain in sin, and therefore separated from God and in the bondage of the evil one. Because the church is God's instrument in preaching the gospel, she finds herself either bitterly opposed by all evil forces or she is tempted to be

sidetracked into all kinds of secondary and social services which in themselves may be good and uplifting, but they do not constitute the essential ministry of the church. Satan never minds a busy church, but he hates a holy and gospel-preaching church because the gospel is "the power of God unto salvation to everyone who believes.

~ G. W. Peters, *A Biblical Theology of Missions*, p. 198.

There is a "Ted Talk" by Simon Senek that has close to ten million views. Simon talks about the Golden Circle which offers an interesting simple insight in to why some corporate organizations have achieved such an exceptional degree of influence. Most corporations think, act, and communicate from the outside in of the Golden Circle. They move from the outer circle of "What (services and products)" to the inner circle, "Why (purpose, cause, or belief)." And for good reason – they go from the tangible to the intangible. In between the outer ring and the inner circle is a middle ring which is "How (how they do it)." Rarely do corporations know or say "Why" they do "What" they do. Let me apply Simon Senek's Golden Circle, to The Church to give us a simple insight to evangelism.

If the Church's purpose, cause, belief (The Why) is souls, then it sets the broad course of action for the "What" and "How" of the Church. The broad course of action for The Church's "What" (services and products) is the Gospel. The broad course of action for the Church's "How" (how they do it) is proclamation/evangelism. Evangelism is not focused on changing behavior. The focus is on changing relationship with God through Jesus Christ. Let the Holy Spirit change behavior. Social action is not to replace the prophetic voice of the church. No matter how feeble that voice is. We do not bring reconciliation/salvation but bring the message of reconciliation/salvation (2 Cor. 5.19-21). We are under the solemn responsibility to make known the unsearchable riches of Christ among the nations.

As a reminder from my Introduction, let me share the needed understanding of the three mandates from God. This understanding will anchor and strengthen you, and the Church, in our primary stewardship. Christians, though strangers and aliens (1 Pet. 2.11), are not excluded from the first mandate which God gave to humanity and that is to be fair by doing justice; to be merciful by doing acts of kindness; and to be humble before God. We would want no less from others, whether saved or unsaved, when we are caught in the unavoidable tragedies of life. We are all bound together as one human race, and we should do unto others as we would want them to do to us. We participate in these no matter what religion is claimed – Christian, Buddhist, Muslim, Hindu, etc. The unsaved and saved are expected to participate in the care of creation and the needs of humanity. Doing this doesn't show the world one is a follower of Jesus let alone communicate the dire reality of God's relationship with sinners and the destiny of their eternal soul. Christians have a different way of showing the world we are followers of Jesus and that is by our love for one another, the second Mandate – "By this all people will know that you are my disciples, if you have love for one another" (John 13.35).

Jesus of Nazareth, the Lord of His Kingdom Society, gave us a new command that he expects us to be obedient too. Our new mandate is in relationship to each other as members of the Kingdom Society. We are to love each other (John 13.34). It is an active, intentional work of love towards the saints as stated in Hebrews 6.10, "For God is not unjust so as to overlook your work and the love that you have shown for his name in serving the saints, as you still do." This serving in the Church, shows no distinction, partiality, or prejudice between the saints, no matter race, status, gender, age, or class. Let the world "see" this inside our own walls and they can't help but know we are Christians, his disciples (John 13.35). What if someone sees our love for each other, and recognizes we are disciples of Jesus, and desires to enter into the Kingdom Society? They aren't morphed in just because the see our love. Someone must proclaim to them the way into this new Kingdom Society or else they will not be able to decide whether they want to enter through the narrow gate (Matt. 7.13-14). This is the third Mandate, which was given to the Church by the risen Lord Jesus (Matt. 28.19-20; Mark 16.15-18; Luke 24.45-49; John 20.21-23; Acts 1.8).

There is only one entrance into the Kingdom Society and that is to confess Jesus is Lord and believe that God has raised Him from the dead (Rom. 10.9). There is justification and salvation in this confessing and believing (Rom. 10.10). Jesus is Lord of all (Rom. 10.12) and therefore all are granted salvation and the riches of the Kingdom Society upon confessing and believing (Rom. 10.12-13). But how can one confess and believe if they have never heard this Good News (Rom. 10.14) and way of entry into eternal life? Someone must open their mouth and share the way into the Kingdom Society.

The commission to the early church was to declare how rebels can enter the blessings of the eternal Kingdom of God – repent and believe on the Lord Jesus Christ. The book of Acts is the story of how the Gospel infiltrated into Jerusalem, Judea, Samaria and the world. It infiltrates through the feet of those who bring this Good News that God in Christ was reconciling the world to Himself not counting men's and women's sins against them. There is no story in Acts where social action for the betterment of Jerusalem, Judea, Samaria, or the world, is demonstrated. The only demonstration of the church tackling an injustice issue is within the church itself (Acts 6). Outside the church walls it's all about the message of forgiveness through faith. Once faith is initiated then there is entry into the Church, where there is a foretaste of the Kingdom of God here and now but not it's fullness. The commission from the Commander in Chief to the troops is, spread the message that victory has been accomplished and to lay down your "arms" and join the winning side – the Kingdom of God. It's the message of the Gospel and the message alone that opens the door into the entrance of His forgiveness, kindness, compassion, blessings – in this world and the world to come.

The severity of the present times and the reality of eternity demands proclamation. We are running out of time. There is only one power greater than the one who has the whole world in his power (1 John 5.19 – "We know that we are from God, and the whole world lies in the power of the evil one.") and that is The Gospel (Rom. 1.16). We have been entrusted with the Gospel, suffer for the Gospel, to go and preach the Gospel, immortality is brought to light through the Gospel (2 Tim. 1.10). A legitimate goal to bring him honor and glory is that all of creation would hear the good news of God in Christ reconciling the world to Himself. All must have an opportunity to know the gospel, all must have representation in the Church of Jesus Christ which is to be gathered from the nations (Acts 19.10; 1 John 2.2; John 3.16-17; John 1.29; Mark 16.15-18, Matt. 28.19, Luke 24.47, Acts 1). The world is our battle ground.

C. S. Lewis wrote, "There is no neutral ground in the universe: every square inch, every split second, is claimed by God and counterclaimed by Satan." What is being claimed and counterclaimed? Is it territory? A "domain?" Yes and no! Yes, all of creation is the Lord's as the rightful King and Lord but it is more than that. It is also, and primarily, the souls that are trapped and in bondage to Satan and his domain like prisoners of war trapped in a concentration camp. He is the prince of the power of the air (Eph. 2.2). He has usurped that which is rightfully God's. All of creation is the Lords for He created all things (Rev. 4.11). There will come a day when all of creation will be restored to the fullness of God's domain

(Rom. 8.19-22). Until then, we must go to our Jerusalem, Judea, Samaria, and the uttermost parts of the world, proclaiming Good News that there is liberation and freedom from Satan's concentration camp of tyranny. We must proclaim, "You are set free in Christ. Walk out of the gate into freedom, wholeness and justice given to you from your Liberator, Jesus Christ."

Only the Church can address and serve one particular need of the world and that is the spiritual need. It is the need of all needs and the cause and root of all the other needs that plague humanity. We must fight to keep this clearly and constantly in mind. Our spiritual enemy will do all he can to sidetrack the Church to labor on the symptoms rather than on the root cause of all needs. The Lord Jesus has called us to meet the deepest need in the soul of each person, the spiritual need, which if not met, has consequences for their eternal destiny either for "weeping and gnashing of teeth" (Matt. 8.12) or for glory (Rom. 5.2). The proclamation of the Gospel is the Church's one tactic to set free the soul that is bound to sin, Satan, and death. It is not proclamation plus demonstration. It is only proclamation. The Gospel proclaimed, through the work of the Holy Spirit, can stand alone. It doesn't need any help at all.

I saw firsthand in Skid Row that the unsaved and the saved can and do meet the endless needs of our hurting and broken world. Clean feet, new socks and a warm meal are needed in Skid Row. In a fallen world I saw humanity at their best doing justly, showing mercy, loving their neighbor as they would want to be loved if they were in the same situation. But this is not missions. Without a verbal proclamation of the Gospel of Jesus Christ, the spiritual forces of darkness will continue to ravage and lock in bondage these souls with their new socks and full belly's. Clean feet, new socks, a warm meal does not get anyone into heaven. Obedient faith to the Gospel of Jesus Christ is the only power to liberate and make a soul into a son or daughter of the King.

Connection:
Rules of Engagement (ROE)

I have focused on the proclamation of the Gospel because I believe this is where the enemy will attack, discourage, twist, and hinder the Church first in the stewardship of the Gospel that has been given to her. But before I move into some practical rules of engagement, lest you think I am unconcerned or, at most, opposed to social justice issues, let me clarify myself.

The Kingdom of God, His rule and reign, has invaded this world and is bringing *freedom*, *wholeness*, and *justice* for all His creation. Everything seen and unseen will at some point in the eternal context of time, submit to His Kingship and rule (Phil. 2.10-11; Rom. 8.19-23) because of the Gospel of Jesus Christ.

When the "seed" of the rule and reign of God enters the "field" of the spirit of the one who believes and confesses that Jesus is the Lord and is alive and risen from the dead (Rom. 10.9), something supernatural takes place in the spiritual realm. They are:

1. Set free from the bondage and tyranny of the Kingdom of Darkness to life and freedom in the Kingdom of God (*freedom*)

2. A new creation in Christ (*wholeness*)

3. Declared not guilty before God (*justice*).

Like a mustard seed it starts small but begins to deepen its roots and grow until it reaches its fullness (Matt. 13.31-32). The individual experiences belonging (1 Cor. 3.23) and identity as a daughter or son of the Most High God, "See what kind of love the Father has given to us, that we should be called children of God; and so we are. The reason why the world does not know us is that it did not know him. Beloved, we are God's children now, and what we will be has not yet appeared; but we know that when he appears we shall be like him, because we shall see him as he is" (1 John 3.1-2).

The person who has experienced the freedom, wholeness, and justice in the spiritual realm of their life is now a citizen of the Kingdom of God and created for good works (Eph. 2.10), that is, to display in word and deed the freedom, wholeness and justice of God's rule and reign. They can be about the debt of love (Rom. 13.8) and be a servant of all to win more to Christ (1 Cor. 9.19). As Peter wrote, we can, "Live as people who are free, not using your freedom as a cover-up for evil, but living as servants of God. Honor everyone. Love the brotherhood. Fear God. Honor the emperor" (1 Pet. 2.16-17). I have walked in this freedom of love and service in many situations:

1. I started a work program for young teen boys in the city by taking them to work at our Morning Star Ranch outside of Wichita, Kansas. They would learn to be on time and with a reasonably good attitude to work and earn money honestly and with dignity.

2. Susan and I have taken into our home young children when the mother was taken off to jail for drugs and family endangerment. The children were uncared for and had lice, which we contracted and had to cut our own hair because of the lice.

3. We had a room added to our home to house teens needing to get out of horrific home situations. They became part of our family.

4. I have fed and served thousands of homeless people in partnership with other ministries.

5. The staff that I directed in Fresno would provide hundreds of Thanksgiving baskets and turkeys for community families living in poverty. We also instituted an annual

Thanksgiving meal in which hundreds would come to the World Impact Center for fellowship, food, and the Gospel.

6. I started the Sonshine Thrift Store to provide clothing and household goods as a means to give a "hand up" by not giving these away but providing these goods at prices those in need could afford without compromising their other financial responsibilities. I'm proud to say that my dad and mom ran the store.

7. We also began a ministry called Sonshine Fashions, where we would bring women newly released from prison to the Sonshine Thrift Store to pick out several pairs of clothes and assist in preparing them for job interviews. These women were released from prison with only their prison garb and nothing else.

8. We also started an annual Christmas store based on the same principle to provide dignity and a hand up and not a handout. We would limit how much a family could spend ($25) so that they wouldn't be tempted towards greed. The prices were drastically reduced on the brand-new toys, clothes, and items. A new basketball might go for $2.

9. Susan helped a young woman to not have an abortion and then walked her through the entire adoption process.

10. I served on the Fresno Chief of Police's Violence Intervention and Community Engagement Task Force.

11. I helped give guidance and support for the first gathering for families who experienced senseless acts of violence in the city. We took them to our World Impact camp to get out of the city and debrief as families in a safe environment.

12. I have served as a Police Chaplain.

I could go on, but the point has been made that social justice is part of and not an empty void in my life. Now let me move into some rules of engagement for The Gospel and Evangelism.

Metrics for an Apostolic Missions Platform – The Gospel
Preparation for an Apostolic Missions Platform – Evangelism

In the Great Commission (Matt. 28.19-20; John 20.21-23; Luke 24.46-48; Mark 16.15-16), in the mandate given by the Lord to His disciples, we find our directions for missions not in meeting endless needs, but in participating in God's purpose to take back souls from the domain of darkness. The Church is to "Go" and keep moving forward into every square inch of this world where a soul has taken refuge and proclaim the gospel of repentance for the forgiveness of sins. Those who respond in obedient faith are to be made into disciples by baptizing them into God's family and teaching them to obey everything of the kingdom domain that is required of children of the King. These baptized followers of the Lord Jesus become the fruit of a new church that raises God's kingdom banner in their community. To get from "going" to "planted" here are several metrics for our Missions Plank, the Gospel, and our Missions Platform task, evangelism.

1. The Gospel Alone

    When assessing our church planters we must be convinced that they are convinced that the Gospel, and the Gospel alone, is the power of God to release souls that are bound in a Kingdom of Darkness and are also convinced that the person who responds in faith is then transferred "to the kingdom of His beloved Son, in whom we have redemption, the forgiveness of sins" (Col. 1.13b-14). For the church planter it is not, "the Gospel plus something else." For them, the Gospel can stand alone without any other help or aid. They wake up each day and know that theirs is the beautiful feet that bring Good News (Isa. 52.7 and Rom. 10.15). They live, breathe, and love the Gospel. If there is any doubt to the priority and place of the Gospel in the church planter's life, vision, and strategy, then the planter should not be authorized at this time for the task of missions.

2. A Gospel Presentation

D. L. Moody was told by a woman, "I don't like the way you do evangelism. He responded with, "I rather don't care for it myself, tell me; how do you do evangelism?" She said, "Well, I don't." He replied, "Well madam, I rather prefer the way I do evangelism versus the way you do not do it." The church planter is well founded in the fact that they are not the bringers of salvation but only the heralds of Good News. Keep moving forward means doing something rather than nothing. The church planter must have a Gospel presentation in which to present. They must know the uncompromising elements in which they can contextualize to reach any culture.

3. I See Souls

Closely related to *The Gospel Alone* is a hunger for souls. They know that souls truly are the currency of the spiritual world. Pastors and assessors will immediately know where the church planters desire is directed. This is observed in the ways I mentioned above:

a. Souls are eternal. They do not believe in annihilationism, i.e., the doctrine that only the righteous live on in immortality and that all others are annihilated; their souls cease to exist.

b. There is a hell. They are not part of the growing trend of "Christians" who do not believe in Hell. They boldly speak on the doctrine of hell no matter how unpopular it is. Since hell is real, the Gospel message and its proclamation is not simply a good option or a cool thing to do but it is literally a matter of life and death.

4. Two Observable Behaviors

There may be more, but, in my observation and experience, these two behaviors rank at the very top for church planters. It is these that push them in their task to proclaim the Gospel of Jesus Christ.

a. Courage is fundamentally the behavior of greatest importance in evangelism. I have shared the Gospel with those who were Crips, Bloods, Nation of Islam, Black Hebrew Israelites, Hindus, Buddhists, poor and rich, male and female, gay and straight, republican and democrat. Courage does not guarantee results but there will definitely be no conversions apart from the courage to evangelize. Remember the words of Winston Churchill: "Success is not final. Failure is not fatal. It is the courage to continue that counts."

b. Angst

The church planter is constantly thinking about the great and awesome day of the Lord (Joel 2.31; Acts 2.20). They walk this uneasy balance of, "no tomorrow," and yesterday is gone. Today must be seized for the Kingdom. Dietrich Bonhoeffer accentuates this angst, "The world dreams of progress, of power, and of the future. But the disciples meditate on the end, the last judgement, and the coming of the Kingdom. To such heights the world cannot rise. And so the disciples are strangers in the world, unwelcome guests and disturbers of the peace. No wonder the world rejects them!" (*The Cost of Discipleship*).

5. Equip Your Church in Evangelism

The Church is the steward of the Gospel and has the responsibility to equip their people in evangelism. Every believer must be able to, "make a defense to anyone who asks you for a reason for the hope that is in you" (1 Pet. 3.15). From this "pool" the pastor can identify those who might have a calling to church plant. There is no church planting without the feet of those who evangelize.

Connection Story

Central City East (official name) in Los Angeles is the homeless capital of America. To Angelenos, it is known as *Skid Row*. The *Independent* (October 2021) gives a graphic picture of this community:

It is estimated that eight thousand homeless people occupy nearly sixty city blocks in downtown LA, living in tents and shabby squalid constructions. Some sleep in the open. Gangs, violence, and drugs run rampant. The rat-infested streets smell of urine and rubbish mixed with the pungent odor of marijuana. Drugs are abundant. "This has become a Disneyland for addicts," one Skid Row resident comments. Heroin, fentanyl, crack, weed and crystal meth are the most popular. Crystal meth, brought in by Mexican cartels and distributed by local gangs in five-dollar bags, is quickly overtaking crack as the drug of choice. "It is Chrys versus Crack, and Chrys is winning," another homeless person wryly comments. . . . Mental illness is rife and half-naked people scream, talk to the air and defecate in the middle of the streets.

In one two-block section you will find every kind of sexual perversion and abuse. It is known as "ho stroll." It is a humanitarian crisis.

It has been some time since I used to evangelize in Skid Row, but much hasn't changed. It is a community where Jesus knows the names of each person who is trapped in the spiritual clutches of the Kingdom of Darkness. His heart weeps for them as He wept over Jerusalem (Luke 19.41). He has not forgotten a single one of them and continues to call saints to proclaim the good news of His love in Jesus His beloved Son. Jennifer is one of those saints.

Jennifer is a petite (at the most 5'5") Taiwanese woman, rejected by her parents and foster parents. She would visit a small church behind her house every Sunday morning where she first began hearing the story of Jesus. "As I grew older, I believed in God but did not attend church or practice my faith at all." When old enough, she married a man who rejected the daughter they had. She left him and came to the United States to build a life for her daughter. As Jennifer states, "My focus was on money and material things, and I took many risks to provide these things for her. One of these risks got me into financial trouble, and then incarceration."

It was in jail that God began to do His work in her to prepare her for the task He had. She doubted her qualifications and ability, thinking it would be impossible for her to be a "Christian leader and soul winner so I cried out to God." Not long after, someone mentioned The Urban Ministry Institute (TUMI), and although we ran a program at the jail for men, we did not have TUMI inside the women's jail. Given our commitment to the least of these, Dr. Bob Lay, our Los Angeles TUMI Satellite Director, personally went down to visit and teach Jennifer (Jennifer graduated from TUMI in 2019 with a *Certificate in Christian Leadership Studies*).

In 2013 Jennifer was released from jail after serving almost two years. Grateful to God, "I knew I needed to serve Him. A friend mentioned Skid Row to me. I didn't know what it was and had never been, so when she brought me there, I couldn't believe the conditions. Immediately I wanted to get involved." She began bringing food and collecting Christian books from all over and would bring them to Skid Row. "I would talk with people in line about Jesus and prayed with them." One day she saw a familiar face among the homeless and called out to him. He was surprised she remembered him. He looked around and said "Did you hear that!? She knows my name!" At that moment, her ministry was born – "Jesus Knows My Name Ministry." Blessing after blessing began to unfold which eventually led Jennifer to attend our Evangel School of Urban Church Planting. Soon after "Church without Walls" was birthed in the heart of Skid Row meeting in an auto repair shop parking lot. The last time I visited this dear sister, I facilitated the Lord's Supper for forty to fifty regular attendees. "I feel this was always God's plan for me. My Chinese name, in fact, translates in English as "Repentance," though I rejected that idea for a long time because of my doubts. There is no denying that God allowed for all these miracles to happen in my life so that "Jesus Knows My Name Ministry" and "Church without Walls" could work to bring more of His children home. God saved me from hopelessness and is now using me to bring hope to a hopeless place."

CHAPTER 4

THE CHURCH: Equip

Key Old Testament Verse

And let them make me a sanctuary, that I may dwell in their midst.

~ Exodus 25

Key New Testament Verse

And when they had appointed elders for them in every church, with prayer and fasting they committed them to the Lord in whom they had believed.

~ Acts 14.23

Contact: Situation Awareness

Monks on Marriage is not your typical book to read. Almost eight years among the urban poor, I began to seek the Lord's will whether to remain single in ministry. I figured monks would have some sage advice on the subject. It was during this season of prayer and journaling that I met Susan. She just finished her Junior year at Taylor University and committed to coming on summer staff with World Impact in 1990. Being a graduate of Taylor I was looking forward to meeting her. When I first saw her in the Wichita office, I said to myself, "Forget *Monks on Marriage*." Susan is beautiful, brave, a risk-taker, creative, mother par excellence, and an incredible wife. It wasn't the monk's advice but the Lord who answered my prayer. Singleness in ministry was not to be.

In August, before she went back to Taylor for her senior year, we were engaged. Susan came back to Wichita after her Fall semester, and we were married February 16, 1991. We took a two-week honeymoon trip out to Fresno California to help restart World Impact's ministry and moved into an area that the police affectionately called "The Devil's Half Mile," or "The Belmont Triangle." Like the stories of the Bermuda Triangle off the eastern tip of Florida in the Atlantic, where ships and aircraft are said to have disappeared under mysterious circumstances, so it was rumored that people have "mysteriously disappeared" in the Belmont Triangle. We called it the Lowell Community after the local Elementary School. It was exactly where the Spirit wanted us to be. Susan finished her degree in social work by serving at the Poverello House, a ministry "serving the hungry, homeless and destitute" and I began to rebuild the mission and vision of World Impact.

We started the ministry with children and youth. It was not long before we had hundreds of children and teens in our weekly Bible Clubs. The World Impact Fresno staff were young, energetic, and sold out to the Gospel and we began to witness the fruits of our prayers and labors. Disciples were being made.

Though these were exciting times these were also very trying times in ministry and family life: a gang member high on drugs shooting at another gang member, on our lawn next to our little girls' window late at night; gangs running after each other and shooting while leading Children's Bible Clubs and having the

children "hit the ground"; being the first and only visitor of a
young man in jail who was in my Bible Club just after he killed
three rival gang members at point blank range; a gang member
shot in the leg on our lawn; a gun pulled out during teen club;
a major gang fight after a teen club in which I was hit in the jaw.
At the time, Fresno was the most violent city per capita, and we
were right in the heart of it all. But how does one make a lasting
change in the "Devils Half-Mile?" Answer: Plant an Outpost of
the Kingdom of God. I didn't really have a specific strategy, but
I did know that we would faithfully continue to evangelize, make
disciples, and begin to bring them together in community. Who
would have thought that a weekly Bible Club would be the tool
the Spirit would use to establish a church among the poor for
His glory?

During our weekly Bible Clubs on our front lawn, I would see
James watching his little boy who attended. He would watch from
the second floor of the house two doors down, as we sang Bible
Club songs, played games, made crafts, and share a story from the
Bible. James never said anything except he would give me that
urban nod of the head recognizing me and that what we were doing
was good for the kids in the neighborhood, even though he was
struggling with drugs and the harshness of the inner city. Something
about the simplicity and purity of children laughing and full of joy
in "The Devil's Half-Mile" could break through the hardest heart.

It was New Year's Day 1996, that I heard a knock and a voice at
our front door early in the morning. It was James my neighbor.
"Bob! We need to talk! Jesus spoke to me last night!" We went
out for breakfast at a neighborhood Mexican restaurant. During
the next several hours, James unfolded his life and the encounter
with the Lord he had that night. There was a true experience
that James had apart from anything I said or did, other than the
Bible Club on our front lawn. I prayed over James, and he prayed

a prayer of faith in Jesus as Lord. Looking at James I said, "You need to be discipled." We set a time for formal discipleship which led to a friendship that continues to this day, though separated by thousands of miles.

Though James had his ups and downs, he began to grow as a disciple. He soon began to invite his community friends to follow Christ and join our weekly fellowship in worship, prayer, and the word. What started as a one-on-one became a one-on-three which became a one-on-nine, which moved to twelve and growing.

At one of our men's group gatherings a local drug addict joined us. He spent a good portion of his time in prison and was known by most everyone in the community. He was my neighbor. It was during this specific night when the Spirit was moving in a powerful way that Tony went into withdrawal and slipped off his chair into convulsions. Immediately the twenty plus men gathered around Tony. Some with arms raised and others laying their hands on Tony, this group of men began praying and believing for a miraculous healing. The Lord answered our prayers. Tony's convulsions stopped immediately, and he quickly rose from the floor, being in his right mind, and joined us in our fellowship. The men gave praise and honor to the Lord Jesus. That week Tony committed and went into a Christian rehab program. This men's group was always a highlight for me. The Spirit was preparing these men to be the foundation of a church plant. The Lord was working in a mighty way.

During this time the Spirit of the Lord brought Pastor Jonathan Villalobos into my life. He, and his wife Becky, felt a strong urge from the Lord to plant a church in the Devil's Half-Mile. His heart and passion for the Lord and the people in this community of poverty and violence, was a confirmation that we were called together to plant a church. As a missionary I knew that I was not called to be a pastor of this church plant. My calling was to decrease and for other leadership to increase and lead the church.

The fall of that year, twenty to thirty men were attending the men's fellowship. Jonathan and I, through much prayer, decided to intentionally establish a church in the Spring of 1997, with Jonathan being the pastor. It was time for this gathering of men to move from a Bible Study to a community of believers committed to worshiping God, growing in the grace and knowledge of the Lord Jesus, and through the Spirit reach out to their neighbors and community with the love of the Gospel. Whosoever will, may come. Easter Sunday, 1997, by the grace of God, Bethany Inner City Church was established and continues to this day to be a beacon of light for the Lowell Community.

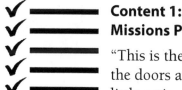

Content 1:
Missions Plank: *The Church*

"This is the church. This is the steeple. Open the doors and see all the people." I learned this little action song while in Sunday School. We would interlock our fingers inwardly and bring our palms and thumbs touching together. "This is the Church." Taking our pointing fingers, we would touch the tips and point them upward. "This is the steeple." To "Open the doors and see all the people" we would open our palms outwardly so that we can see our fingers and thumbs and wiggle them to imitate the people.

I love the Church. As a child, it was in the Church that I came to believing faith in Jesus the Lord. I have fond memories of Sunday evenings when it was Special Hymn Night. When asked for a favorite hymn I would shoot my hand up and shout out page 63 without even being called upon. Yes, I still remember the page number for "The Old Rugged Cross." There was something about the chorus that touched me as a child:

So, I'll cherish the old, rugged cross
Till my trophies at last I lay down
And I will cling to the old, rugged cross
And exchange it some day for a crown

It still touches me some fifty years later. I remember grandmas giving me a big smile, pinching my checks while giving me some hard candy to suck on during church. We had no cell phones or electronic games in Sunday School, but we had flannel graph. A wonder of wonders. As a child I was mesmerized at how the figures just stuck to the board as the Sunday School teacher told the Bible story. We sang, ate, laughed, cried, worked, prayed, and evangelized. We had friends. It was family. It was a place of belonging. I love the Church.

I grew up in the 60s and 70s. Not to take a long trip down memory lane but life was simpler back then. Words and phrases were clear in their meaning. Everyone knew exactly what was meant. We knew when a fight was going to break out when you heard someone say, "Yo mama!" No one used "Yo Uncle" or "Yo niece" as fighting words. It was "Yo mama" that you knew the fisticuffs was about to take place. You never, ever brought someone's mama onto the scene without taking the risk of the consequences. You were going to defend your mama if it cost you a bloody nose or a black eye.

Cyprian was an early Christian theologian and bishop of Carthage who led the Christians of North Africa during a period of persecution from Rome. He wrote *The Unity of the Church*, which is considered his greatest work. In it he states, "No one can have God for his Father, who does not have the Church for his mother." The urban hood translation according to Dr. Davis is, "If the Church ain't yo mama then God ain't yo Daddy." If Cyprian is correct, and I believe he is, then those who call upon

THE CHURCH: EQUIP • 143

God as Father must love the Church. They must love, defend, and speak well of the Community of the Kingdom.

In our present Western society, there is a general feeling that "I can do without the Church," by many "Christians," let alone the secular culture. This could be from a variety of reasons – physical and verbal abuse by those in church authority; the hypocrisy of church leaders who preach one thing and do the other; greed for money and the things of this world; misunderstanding; cliques; pride. As someone once said, "The Church is like Noah's ark. If it weren't for the storm outside, we couldn't stand the funk on the inside."

Yes, the Church has a sordid past and present, and will continue this way into the future until the Lord returns. Bad players have been and will continue to be within her midst. There will always be tares among the wheat (Matt. 13.24-30). This is the infiltrating work of Satan and his demonic forces (2 Cor. 11.14-15). He hates the Bride of Christ. He will use anyone and anything to malign and destroy the Church. His hatred and wrath know no bounds, for he is well aware of who the Church is:

1. The Church is an outpost of the Kingdom of God. In war, a military outpost is a detachment of troops positioned to stand guard against unauthorized intrusions and surprise attacks. They provide protection to an area. Apply this definition to a local church and you have a detachment of disciples under the rule and reign of God Almighty standing guard against the forces of darkness. Does a local church see herself this way? Ed Silvoso doesn't think so. In his book, That None Should Perish he said, "The Church in the West today presents too easy a target for Satan. We do not believe we are at war. We do not know where the battleground is located, and in spite of our weapons, they are neither loaded nor aimed at the right target. We are unaware of how vulnerable we are. We are better fitted

for a parade than for an amphibious landing." Strong words but worth meditating upon, considering the times in which we live.

2. The Church is the agent of God's Kingdom witness. Ephesians 3.10 states, "so that through the church the manifold wisdom of God might now be made known to the rulers and authorities in the heavenly places." The Church witnesses through joyful obedience to the rule and reign of God. Jesus is the rightful King of God's Kingdom, and we kneel before Him in gratitude and readiness to serve Him even unto the point of death. When we pray, "Thy Kingdom come Thy will be done" (Matt. 6.10), we are praying that my kingdom and my will be gone. I am no longer on the throne of my life as the ruler who is seeking my will and desires. This is the witness that is seen and confounds the created beings in the spiritual world and frustrates and condemns those in the world (Acts 5.27-33). The Church is the only agent in this world that demonstrates submission to the redemptive rule and reign of God and His Kingdom. The Lord is calling out to the Church today, "CAN I GET A WITNESS?"

3. The Church is the pillar and foundation of the truth (1 Tim. 3.15). The Church has an ancient history founded on the pillars of truth. She defends a Great Tradition, our Sacred Roots. This Great Tradition represents the core of our Christian faith and practice from the apostles who passed it down to our church fathers. We are part of a rich legacy of eternal treasures that the Church has always confessed and believed, a worship that has been undivided, celebrated and embodied through the Lords Supper, and a mission that it has embraced and sacrificed for. "All possible care must be taken, that we hold that faith which

has been believed everywhere, always, by all" (Vincent of Lerins, fifth-century monk).

4. The Church is the sign of God's covenant faithfulness. The Bible is the story of the one true God, redeeming (Titus 2.14) and reconciling (2 Cor. 5.17) His enemies (Rom. 5.10) to Himself because of His abounding love, grace and mercy. Through the willful disobedience of our first parents the rebellion began. The world and all who would dwell upon it, were cursed and corrupted leading to the only inevitable outcome – separation, death, pain and sorrow. None could escape. All would be bound and shackled in a spiritual domain of darkness with no hope. God, in His great love and mercy though, made a covenant promise in the presence of these two convicted rebels and the Serpent, that Satanic deceiver (Gen. 3.15). From that moment on God announced and began to initiate His liberation plan. At the appointed time He would send His anointed authorized person to usher in the dawn of a new age of God's redemptive rule and reign (Gal. 4.4-6). Jesus of Nazareth, born of the Virgin Mary, was the person of the covenant promise from the Garden of Eden. He entered into the spiritual war announcing, "The time is fulfilled, and the Kingdom of God is at hand. Repent and believe in the Gospel" (Mark 1.15). It was the beginning of the end. All those who would turn and believe in this Gospel of Jesus would form God's new Kingdom Society of the "called out ones" – the Church. The Church is the sign of God's covenant faithfulness announced in the Garden of Eden.

5. The Church is the foretaste of God's kingdom blessing. God is good (Ps. 145.9) and the giver of every perfect gift (James 1.17). Though we have not yet experienced the fullness of God's kingdom blessings we do experience a

taste of it now. In this age of the "Not yet, Already Kingdom" we experience these divine realities from our Great God and His Victorious Son:

a. Our fundamental disposition is transformed. We have peace with God (Col. 1.20) rather than His wrath (Col. 3.6)

b. We are cleansed from sin and unrighteousness (1 John 1.7-10)

c. We have been rescued and delivered from the bondage of the Kingdom of Darkness (Col. 1.13)

d. We have been redeemed and forgiven (Col. 1.14)

e. We have been redeemed from the curse of the law (Gal. 3.13)

f. The nature of God is imparted to us (2 Pet. 1.4)

g. The image of Christ is recreated in us (Rom. 8.29)

h. We are made a child of God (1 John 3.1)

i. We receive the precious gift of the Holy Spirit that we can live a life of true discipleship (John 14-15-31)

6. The Church is the co-heir of God's exalted King – Jesus Christ. Romans 8.17 says, "Now if we are children, then we are heirs – heirs of God and co-heirs with Christ, if indeed we share in his sufferings in order that we may also share in his glory." As His children, we have "an inheritance that can never perish, spoil or fade . . . kept in heaven" (1 Pet. 1.4). In other words, as His children (John 1.12), we have inheritance rights. We are His beneficiaries and therefore qualified to, "share in the inheritance of the saints in light (Col. 1.12). Jesus is the "heir" as the Son of God (Matt. 3.17; 2 Pet. 1.17)

and has been appointed the heir of all things (Heb. 1.2).
We are co-heirs because of our adoption as His children.
As co-heirs we share in the inheritance of Jesus. Everything
that is Jesus's, belongs to us. We must not throw away our
confidence in this as there is a great reward (Heb. 10.35).
We must endure (Heb. 10.36).

7. The Church is a steward, a custodian of the power of God
. . . the Gospel. The Church is the custodian of the keys
of the Kingdom of God (Matt. 16.19). A key opens and
locks doors. They represent authority, responsibility, and
trust from the one who gives the keys to the one who
receives the keys. The Church acts on behalf of the Lord
Jesus to either set men free by the proclamation of the
Gospel or keeping them bound by locking up their voice.
Only the Church has the keys to unlock the power of
the Gospel through her proclamation that, "in Christ God
was reconciling the world to himself, not counting their
trespasses against them" (2 Cor. 5.19a). We have been
entrusted to steward this message of reconciliation
(2 Cor. 5.19b). The stewardship of this proclamation
is a tremendous responsibility the Church has toward
the world. If the church fails, no one else can unlock the
power of God, and the world will remain condemned,
damned, separated from God and in the bondage of the
evil one. The Church can either bind or lose depending
on how they function in their custodianship (Matt. 18.18).
As the steward and the custodian of the keys of the
Kingdom of God and the unsearchable riches that are
in Christ (Eph. 3.8), we must go to the nations and
preach the power of God unto salvation to every creature
(Mark 16.15).

8. The Church is the Church Militant. The Devil is relentless
and ruthless. He shows no mercy and seeks only to kill,
steal, and destroy. He is a tyrant who is totally depraved.

His sick evil ways know no bounds. There is no good in him. He hates the Church and will never stop his onslaught against her. This doesn't even begin to dive into the depths of this created angel bent on nothing less than the overthrow of God, His Kingdom, and the saints who have been rescued from the clutches of this prince of the power of the air. Just a small understanding of this, one can understand why the Church must be militant. Our battle is not against flesh and blood but against the rulers, against the authorities, against the cosmic powers over this present darkness, against the spiritual forces of evil in the heavenly places (Eph. 6.12). We need to be aggressive, violent, combative, and confrontational towards the sin which can so easily entangle us (Heb. 12.1). Notice how it tells "us" this, and not the world. We are not to be this – aggressive, violent, combative, and confrontational towards the world. They are already entangled in sin and under the wrath of God. The only means and power in which to untangle them and appease God's wrath is the Gospel of peace.

By militant I also mean that we must be aggressively moving forward in missions to expand and advance God's Kingdom in enemy occupied territory. We must not let sin, Satan or the world hinder us. Our cause is to honor and glorify God in the spiritual war we were born into, knowing that the enemy will never stop.

The Church is the Community of the Kingdom but never the Kingdom itself. The Kingdom is God's reign and the realm in which the blessings of his reign are experienced; the church is the fellowship of those who have experienced God's rule and reign and entered the enjoyment of its blessings. The Kingdom creates the church, works through the church, and is proclaimed in the world by the church. The Church is the end game in town. Is your faith deep enough to believe this about the Church, no matter how small or poor that gathered Community is? Roland Allen said this in his book, *The Spontaneous Expansion of the Church*, "What is necessary is faith. What is needed is the kind of faith which uniting a man to Christ, sets him on fire. Such a man can believe that others finding Christ will be set on fire also. Such a man can see there is no need of money to fill a continent with the knowledge of Christ. Such a man can see that all that is required to consolidate and establish that expansion is the simple application of the simple organization of the Church. It is to men who know that faith, who see that vision, that I appeal. Let them judge what I have written."

Content 2:
"E" of an Apostolic Missions Platform: *Equipping*

It is no surprise then, that within the history of missions, the devil and his forces have sought nothing more than to malign and destroy the Church. He has, and continues to be, relentless and ruthless in his efforts. He has been at it since the first day of the Church's founding. He knows that any attempt of his, even though his hellish gates will not prevail (Matt. 16.18), could hinder and cease all efforts of the responsibility of the, ". . . apostles, the prophets, the evangelists, the shepherds and teachers, to equip the saints for the work of ministry, for building up the body of Christ, until we all attain to the unity of the faith and of the knowledge of the Son of God, to mature manhood, to the measure of the stature of the fullness of Christ, so that we may no longer be children, tossed to and fro by the waves and carried about by every wind of doctrine, by human cunning, by craftiness in deceitful schemes. Rather, speaking the truth in love, we are to grow up in every way into him who is the head, into Christ, from whom the whole body, joined and held together by every joint with which it is equipped, when each part is working properly, makes the body grow so that it builds itself up in love" (Eph. 4.11-16). If saints are not equipped, "through and for" the Church, then the spread of the Gospel and the multiplication efforts of the Church's mission will falter and may altogether come to a halt, leading to the body of Christ not being built up. The equipping task of the Church is critical in our *Apostolic Missions Platform*.

Equipping the saints is not an option nor just for some. All those who claim Christ Jesus as Lord enter His service in this cosmic spiritual battle between the Kingdom of God and the Kingdom of Darkness. Allegiance to the Lord, through confession of obedient faith by grace, automatically enlists them to make disciples and to fan into flame the gift which God has given them, in order to, "make the body grow so that it builds itself up in love" (Eph. 4.16). This is not a service of violence as the world knows violence but an aggression of unrelenting love that seeks the salvation of all for the glory of God. It is a love that is, "patient and kind; it does not envy or boast; it is not arrogant or rude. It does not insist on its own way; it is not irritable or resentful; it does not rejoice at wrongdoing but rejoices with the truth. It bears all things, believes all things, hopes all things, endures all things. It is a love that never ends" (1 Cor. 4-8a). It is *"The Mark of a Christian"* (Title to Francis Shaeffer's spiritual classic). With this mark, this identification, spiritual leadership within the Church, equip the saints in disciple making and gift development. Let's look at these two areas of leadership equipping: disciple making and gift development.

Disciple Making

We all know the Great Commission, especially the one quoted in Matthew 28.19-20, "Go therefore and make disciples of all nations, baptizing them in the name of the Father and of the Son and of the Holy Spirit, teaching them to observe all that I have commanded you. And behold, I am with you always, to the end of the age." The command to *Go*, in the Greek as used here, is a participle and conveys the idea to "go along the routine of your daily life." *Disciple* in the Greek, as used here, is a verb in the aorist imperative second person plural. Basically, what this is communicating is a critical command, "You, you keep on discipling without any stopping." This verb differs from the parent verb in that it describes the dedication of a student. Some have said that Jesus's command is to "enthuse" others into becoming students of Jesus. Putting these insights together, the Great Commission could be stated, "As you're going through the routine of your life, wherever that is, your work-place, the neighborhood you live, the places you visit and hang out, in these places, enthuse others about Me. Don't ever stop. Keep at it to the very end. Disciple them by baptizing and teaching them everything I have commanded you. I am the Lord, and I'll be with you in your going, your baptizing, your teaching, until it's all said and done." Understanding Jesus's command like this means, everyone who claims allegiance to Jesus, must engage in His Great Commission to go, disciple, baptize, and teach. This command of the Lord Jesus is not only for the ordained and commissioned, but it includes all who claim allegiance to Jesus. Everyone is called to engagement in the advancement of God's Kingdom – girls and boys, teens, moms and dad, grandmas and grandpas, single or married, working or unemployed, healthy or struggling in health, in season and out of season.

This begs two fundamental questions that need to be answered. The first one, "when is a disciple made?" In other words, is there a "completion" a "final product" in the making process in which one can look and say, "There's a disciple of Jesus!" The second question is, "how long does it take to make a disciple?" Is this an open-ended disciple making process or is there some sort of general time frame in which to guide me as I make disciples? Let me start with the first question, "when is a disciple made?"

Foundationally, one becomes a convert when the person hears the Good News of what God has done in Christ Jesus and responds, through faith (Eph. 2.8), to the conviction of the Holy Spirit (John 16.8). Remember, the one proclaiming is just a messenger and has no power to convert. That is the work of the Holy Spirit and His alone.

But the mandate is not to make a convert but to make a disciple. How do we equip, that is – "to supply with the necessary items for a particular purpose" (Oxford Dictionary) – the convert who confesses Jesus is Lord and believes He is risen and alive (Rom. 10.9) so that others can see that their conversion is authentic by their following the One in whom they have converted to? What are the necessary items we are to supply so that the disciple can demonstrate a faith that brings spiritual fruit with repentance (Matt. 3.8)? According to the Great Commission in Matthew, there are two equipping items in which we disciple a convert to be a disciple of Jesus. We equip them by supplying baptism and teaching them everything Jesus commanded. The convert's responsibility is to submit and obey.

The first equipping item we supply is baptism (Matt. 28.19). This onetime act is more than a symbolic washing away of known sin; it is a baptism into the Lord Jesus. It demonstrates that the convert has been crucified with Christ, buried with Him in His death, and now is risen to new life as a child of God and is translated into the Kingdom Society. This sacrament is one of the greatest joys of the participant and those who witness the experience. If the disciple maker does not supply the sacrament of baptism to the one confessing their allegiance to the Lord Jesus, they are not equipping the convert. They have fallen short of the Lord's command to make a disciple.

The second equipping item the disciple maker supplies is to teach them to observe everything that Jesus taught the disciples as recorded in the Gospels (Matt. 28.20). When supplying this for the convert it allows them to demonstrate their submission and obedience to the Lord Jesus. Remember, the convert is to submit and obey to their new Lord. If the one making a disciple is to supply the convert with everything that Jesus taught us, so that they can demonstrate obedience to the One they are now claiming to be their Lord, what is "everything" so that the disciple maker can fulfill the Lords Great Commission mandate? Is there a radical minimum to "everything" that Jesus taught?

Dr. George Patterson trained pastors and planted churches in Central America, where his strategies for church multiplication became known. He asked himself the same question and came up with the "Seven Basic Commands of Christ" found in the New Testament. In his context, most of the new converts were illiterate. He taught them orally the seven basic commands of Christ, with the pertinent Scripture texts for them to memorize. They memorized the key texts so effectively and thoroughly, that they were able to witness to others by reciting the verses without usually having the ability to read them. The Seven Basic Commands of Christ according to Patterson are as follows:

1. Confess, repent, and believe the Gospel (Mark 1.15).

2. Be baptized and receive the Holy Spirit (Matt. 28.19; Acts 2.38).

3. Love

   a. God (Matt. 22.37)

   b. Neighbor (any other person irrespective of race or religion with whom we live or whom we chance to meet) (Matt. 22.39)

   c. One another (those in the Kingdom Society; brothers and sisters in Christ) (John 13.34)

4. Celebrate the Lord's Supper (Luke 22.17-20).

5. Pray (Matt. 6.5-15).

6. Give (Matt. 16.19-21; Matt. 10.8).

7. Go and disciple (Matt. 28.18-20).

Truly, there are more than seven commandments that were given by Jesus. Some have counted over 30. This is not a legalistic exercise but an honest look for us to be obedient to Christ's command to make disciples by, "teaching them everything I have commanded you." These are seven "basic commands" in which Jesus's other commands fit, or closely fit into.

We now can answer our question, "when is a disciple made?" If, we apply what Jesus commanded for us to do, that is, baptize and teach, using the seven basic commands of Christ, we can look at the person and determine if the discipling process is completed: they have confessed, repented and believed in the Gospel; they were baptized and filled with the Holy Spirit; they are loving God, their neighbor and the Church Community; they celebrate the Lord's Supper; they pray; they give; they go and disciple by following the same pattern. "There is a disciple of Jesus." This is not a subjective process but an objective one. It's not based on feelings but on clear observable demonstrations of obedience.

Discipleship is a lifetime journey of obedience though (John 14.15). Disciples fall short of the glory of God, but God is faithful when the disciple isn't faithful (2 Tim. 2.13) and He continues His purpose to conform the disciple into the image of Jesus (Rom. 8.29), each step of the way. "Discipleship, therefore, must necessarily be an uncomfortable process of reorientation and of abandonment of the self-centered values of human society in favor of the divine economy" (Ladd). As disciple makers, we can water (spiritualize – baptize) and we can plant (spiritualize – teach) but only God can cause the growth (1 Cor. 3.5-9). This is the "radical minimum" to equip a convert so that they can demonstrate they are a disciple of their Lord and Savior, Jesus.

The second question is a time question. How long does this take? A day? A week? A month? Nine months? Forever? Scripture doesn't give us a definitive answer. What I can say with confidence over the years of equipping converts who became disciples of the Lord is, "one time frame doesn't fit all." Let me share a biblical example to get us thinking.

Paul and Barnabas are commissioned and released by the Church in Antioch for the task of missions, "The sending forth of authorized persons to unchurched communities to proclaim the Gospel in order to win converts to Jesus Christ, make disciples from the converts, and gather together the disciples to form functioning, multiplying local churches, that bear the fruit of the Kingdom of God in that community." Here is what we know from their first journey: they made disciples at Antioch in Pisidia (Acts 13.52; 14.21-22), disciples in Iconium (Acts 14.1; 21-22), disciples in Lystra (Acts 14.20), and disciples in Derbe (Acts 14.20-21), with the intent of establishing a "functioning, multiplying local congregation/church" led by appointed elders (Acts 14.23).

What we don't know exactly is whether Paul and Barnabas adhered strictly to the seven basic commands. They definitely had a process though or else it wouldn't have been recorded that, disciples were made in these cities, from their first journey. It's not far out of reach to think that they baptized, and taught a radical minimum of what demonstrated to Paul and Barnabas the converts obedience to the commands of the Lord Jesus Christ. We also know a basic timeline for Paul and Barnabas's first journey which was about a year, maybe two. Considering the time, it took to travel by ship and by walking, and then turning back around to retrace their steps to these cities, they were confident that disciples were made and that fully functioning, multiplying churches were established, bearing fruit of the Kingdom of God in those cities.

Here's the encouraging point: It didn't take years for the Apostle Paul and Barnabas to make disciples and congregate them into new churches in a hostile, pagan world, while on their first missions journey. They entrusted the disciples that were made, and had gathered in small churches, to the Holy Spirit and the appointed Elders.

Gift Development

Gift development is different than making disciples of Jesus. Though the word isn't used in the New Testament specifically, it is apprenticeship. Apprenticing is the process of identifying, equipping, commissioning, and releasing disciples in the calling and gifting the Spirit of the Lord has divinely given them for the building up of the body of Christ. It is the principle of reproducing "in kind." Apply this "in kind" principle to the five-fold gifts and you have the following:

1. Called and gifted apostolic individuals apprentice called and gifted apostolic individuals.

2. Called and gifted prophetic individuals apprentice called and gifted prophetic individuals.

3. Called and gifted evangelists apprentice called and gifted evangelists.

4. Called and gifted shepherds/pastors apprentice called and gifted shepherds/pastors.

5. Called and gifted teachers apprentice called and gifted teachers.

The same is true for all the other gifts the Spirit gives to the saints. In its most rudimentary form, an apprentice within the Kingdom, is a disciple who is developing their spiritual gift from a mature skilled disciple who has the same spiritual gift. Combining the rigors of hard intellectual study, practical experience, and supervised feedback, apprenticeships are a powerful and effective way to multiply leaders capable of producing tangible results for mission and bringing health and vitality to the church. We can powerfully equip qualified emerging leaders to become godly, effective servants of Christ for missions. By emphasizing good selection, careful and capable supervision, meaningful assignments, and regular feedback, we can help emerging, developing, and mature movements gain invaluable training to expand and advance the Kingdom of God in their context. Let's take a closer look at the apprenticing process: Identify. Equip. Commission. Release.

Identification

In Luke 6.12-16 we read the following story, "In these days he went out to the mountain to pray, and all night he continued in prayer to God. And when day came, he called his disciples and chose from them twelve, whom he named apostles: Simon, whom he named Peter, and Andrew his brother, and James and John, and Philip, and Bartholomew, and Matthew, and Thomas, and James the son of Alphaeus, and Simon who was called the Zealot, and Judas the son of James, and Judas Iscariot, who became a traitor." Jesus, "the apostle and high priest of our confession (Heb. 3.1), identifies, from a group of disciples, twelve whom He was going to apprentice to be apostles. Jesus follows the laws of His creation by "reproducing in kind." An apostle apprenticing apostles.

When apprenticing potential called and gifted individuals for missions, it is important, that apostolic called and gifted individuals seek the Spirits direction to identify those with whom they are going to equip for missions. This is different than making disciples by proclaiming the Gospel through the routine of our daily life and, those who convert because of the conviction of the Holy Spirit, are equipped through baptism and in teaching them to obey what Jesus has commanded. When an apostolic individual is identified through prayer and the confirmation of the Holy Spirit, the one with the apostolic gift gives them their time, talent, and treasure, to mature their gift, towards to end of commissioning and releasing them in missions – "the sending forth of authorized persons to unchurched communities to proclaim the Gospel in order to win converts to Jesus Christ, make disciples from the converts, and gather together the disciples to form functioning, multiplying local churches, that bear the fruit of the Kingdom of God in that community." Like Jesus, who had the multitudes (Matt. 4.25; John 6.2), the hundred and twenty (Acts 1.15), the seventy (Luke 10), the twelve (Matthew 10.2-4) and the three (Matt. 17.1), so we also must distinguish between those we are going to give our time and resource investment for the purpose of apprenticing in missions. There is no guarantee that you will not have a Judas in the midst. Move forward with who you feel the Spirit has identified for you to apprentice. Remember, this is not equipping to make a disciple, but to identify those whom to apprentice, in our case, for missions, keeping in mind that like reproduces in kind.

Individuals must already possess the radical minimum of maturity and experience as a disciple of Jesus in order to be considered worthy for either, 1) equipping for the ministry in the local church, or 2) to equip them for the planting of new churches (missions). Great care and focus must be done in advance to guarantee its success. It was Barnabas who identified Paul and brought him to the Church in Antioch for a year of equipping (Acts 11.25-26). The Apostle Paul, though called and gifted by the Lord Jesus Himself while on the road to Damascus, still submitted himself to the leadership of the local church in Antioch. When the equipping was completed, the elders in Antioch, through the Holy Spirit, commissioned Paul and Barnabas, "for the work to which I (the Holy Spirit) called them" and then released them for the Kingdom task given to them. That is why equipping is "from and for" the church.

Equipping

After Jesus identified the twelve disciples (not converts), he designates them as apostles (Mark 3.14) and begins a three-year apprenticeship program to equip them as apostles. After His resurrection, He speaks to the Apostles for forty days (Acts 1.2) about the Kingdom of God (Acts 1 3). This would complete their apprenticeship as apostles, "sent ones." Jesus equipped his apprentices for missions.

The goal of apprenticeship is to hone – refine, grind, sharpen, file - the disciple, who has the same gift as the one apprenticing, to bring their gift to maturity, in order to represent the Kingdom of God in excellence and confidence for building up of the Body of Christ whether in ministry or missions. We must apprentice them in fanning into flame the vision and the gift that the Holy Spirit has given them (1 Cor. 12.4). So, what are some practical principles and marks to apprentice someone towards confidence and excellence in the gift given them by the Holy Spirit?

The thoughts that I share are from a resource from The Urban Ministry Institute: *Becoming Like Your Teacher: Developing Effective Church Planting Apprenticeships*. There is a wealth of biblical, theological, and practical insights from this resource. For the purposes of this booklet, I'm going to pull out the "four non-negotiable principles" that will strengthen the "six clear marks/targets" so that in partnership with the Holy Spirit, leadership can commission, that is, "to set apart" (Acts 13.2), the individual who has completed their apprenticeship.

Equipping in a wise supervised apprenticeship program is an effective means to multiply spiritual laborers for the harvest, and to equip servant-leaders for effective ministry through and for the church. The following four principles are essential for a well-designed apprentice program. Though each has equal

weight, individuals who are identified will come at various levels
of maturity and development, i.e., in their overall understanding
of Scripture, ministry experience, Christ-centered life. That is
why the focus needs to be on the principles of apprenticeship.
From these principles you can make a tailor-made apprentice
program to equip the identified individual.

Principle #1 – Leadership Development. "Survival of the fittest is
not the same as survival of the best. Leaving leadership development
up to chance is foolish" (Morgan McCall). Designing your
leadership development track requires prayer and intentionality.
One size does not fit all. Leaders are made, not born. You must
know your apprentice and what they need to make them into
a leader.

Principle #2 – Biblical and Theological Training. "As we have said
before, so now I say again: If anyone is preaching to you a gospel
contrary to the one you received, let him be accursed" (Gal. 1.9).
From the beginning of history, the enemy has sought to twist and
malign God's word. A half-truth is always a full lie. The Church's
history is filled with women and men who sacrificed their lives for
the defense of the Church's confession, what it has "believed
everywhere, always and by all." A solid apprenticeship program
respects and demands this; a good one always has a quality
biblical and theological training component.

Principle #3 – Experience (Field Work/Boots on the Ground).
"And he appointed twelve (whom he also named apostles) *so that
they might be with him,* and he might send them out to preach"
(Mark 3.14). Designing the experience part of the training will
depend on the calling and gifting (ministry or missions) of the
individual. In either case, an apprentice is not just about books
to read and assignments to be completed. The best apprenticeships
must include the seasoned leader (with the same gift) personally
investing into the apprentice with the same calling and gifting.
Jesus the Apostle (Heb. 3.1) apprenticed His apostles by having

them be with Him and watch Him do the miraculous and proclaim the message of the Kingdom. He gave them ministry. He worshiped and prayed with them, and He taught them. And when tough issues needed to be addressed, Jesus addressed them clearly and kept the Apostles accountable. He was developing and sharpening their calling and gift as authorized sent ones for missions. There is simply no substitute for experience from the guidance of the leader with the apprentice.

Principle #4 – Spiritual Growth (Endearment). "Therefore, let us leave the elementary doctrine of Christ and go on to maturity, not laying again a foundation of repentance from dead works and of faith toward God" (Heb. 6.1). God expects each of his children to mature in Christ, to develop into full adults in Him. Like our own children, such maturity will not happen overnight nor by chance. Good loving parental care is intentional. Such care provides input for the purpose of maturity, and it necessarily implements the refining responsibilities along each of life's growth stages. Just like a developing child, in similar fashion, an apprentice needs the necessary spiritual formation to grow, strengthen, and mature in the gift they have been given. Spiritual maturity is essential for each one who feels called to serve the Commander of the Lords Army in every situation.

These are the four principles that every apprenticeship program must be comprised of. Once your apprenticeship program has been designed and the equipping has begun, there are six marks that the one who is apprenticing needs to constantly keep before them as a target for the apprentice.

Mark/Target #1 – Master the art and discipline of being a worthy leader. There are many qualities for effective leadership that are mentioned in books, the internet, conferences on leadership, such as: integrity, ability to delegate, self-awareness, gratitude, empathy, respect, honesty, creativity, humility, courage, and others. I have found personally that the following qualities to be indispensable in apprenticing church planters and emerging leaders of church plant movements.

   a. *Listening.* As I mentioned on the apostolic missions plank, the Holy Spirit, there is no missions apart from His leading. Leadership requires the discipline to hone ones listening skills to hear from the Holy Spirit. When apprenticing church planters and movement leaders I have two primary agenda items: 1) what is the Spirit of the Lord speaking to you about, and 2) what is on your agenda. It's not that I don't have things that are on my agenda, but these two agenda questions require me to listen before speaking. I want to hear that they are hearing from the Spirit, and what is on their agenda is more important than what is on mine. James wants all men and women to be quick to listen (James 1.19). How much more the leader.

   b. *Communication.* Napoleon Bonaparte, the French military leader, and emperor who conquered much of Europe in the early nineteenth century said, "The secret of war lies in the communication." Our prayer communication with God, in this spiritual war, is meant to be a walkie-talkie, calling down fire on enemy positions on a battlefield where all is at stake. Our communication with our co-laborers, in this spiritual war, must be clear, regular, and honest. This quality in the apprentice must be refined as it is the secret in the expansion and advancement of God's Kingdom in the spiritual war, we find ourselves in.

   c. *Polytetrafluoroethylene (PTFE).* You would know this by the brand name, Teflon. In leadership, when the rains of life and ministry come and the floods rise all around, when the irritations from the spiritual enemy are grating your inner spirit raw, and when the unbelievable and unforeseen attacks against you, your family, and the vision

God has given you are almost unbearable, the leader needs to have an inner Teflon coating (waterproof, frictionless, and nonstick). You have to see this in the apprentice and speak into it. It must be strengthened, for the enemy will challenge it, condemn it, and do all he can to crush it. An authentic spiritual Teflon in leaders, keeps them from "not shrinking back" from the task given them for Kingdom advancement and expansion. I'm not talking about a false or perfect coating for it is still the daily grace of God that is our sufficiency and His power that is perfected in our weakness (2 Cor. 12.9).

d. *Submission.* I speak on this in the ROE section below.

Mark/Target #2 – Engage in personal evangelism and spiritual warfare. The apprentice must know how to engage in evangelism that leads the hearer to a point of response, whether yah or nah. Engaging spiritual warfare through prayer will be foundational (Rom 1.16; Eph. 6.18).

Mark/Target #3 – Follow up new Christian converts and disciple them. The apprentice must know how to lead a convert to be a disciple of Jesus. He/she must be skilled in doing this. They need to know how to baptize and teach what baptism signifies in the converts life. They need to be skilled in teaching the convert the commands of Jesus. The seven basic commands of Christ are a good place to start. It is interesting that the only non-character trait that is required of an elder is the ability to teach (2 Tim. 2.24).

Mark/Target #4 – Do the work of a pastor, shepherding others and fulfilling pastoral responsibilities. The apprentice must have the necessary gifts, character, and skills to "shepherd the flock."

Mark/Target #5 – Understand and be committed to the principles of spiritual reproduction and church planting movements. There must be clear observation and communication from the apprentice that, "none should perish." The apprentice must understand the vastness of the harvest field and the importance of reproduction and multiplying themselves to create disciples and church planting movements (2 Tim. 2.2; 1 Thess. 1.8). They need to be able to disciple and apprentice.

Mark/Target #6 – Possess a strategic vision for contributing to the Great Commission, and a practical plan to implement it. The apprentice must have a vision from the Lord that burns within and a plan to unleash this Spirit given vision.

Jesus knew that, in and of themselves, the apostles could not meet the expectations Jesus had. His Kingdom advancement and expansion is a worldwide vision and mission. They would need a power, not of this world. A divine, supernatural power. Jesus needed to implant His very own Spirit within them in order for them to receive power and rise-up to the commission He had given them. So, Jesus, "ordered them not to depart from Jerusalem, but to wait for the promise of the Father, which, he said, "you heard from me; for John baptized with water, but you will be baptized with the Holy Spirit not many days from now" (Acts 1.4-5). This would be their commissioning for missions.

Comissioning

Commissioning usually involves a service in which the laying on of hands takes place upon the individual. Sometimes prayer and fasting precedes and/or accompanies this time (Acts 13.3). Though the individual has already received the Holy Spirit, the laying on of hands in the commissioning service is associated with the recognition that he/she needs the power of the Holy Spirit for the responsibility given them by the Holy Spirit. It is a conferral of authority that Church leadership affirms for the task that they have been identified and equipped to accomplish (See Acts 6.6; 13.3; and 1 Tim. 4.14) for the building up of the Body of Christ (Eph. 4.12).

The individual is now *RELEASED* with full authority to go and do that which they have been identified, apprenticed, and commissioned to do. To be released is to be "sent off" and not "sent away." The commissioning authority, gives authority, to move forward and multiply. The individual is not to be "managed" but to be "regulated." In other words, the individual will report back to the sending authority, but the individual does not take orders from it. He/she has been commissioned and will now begin to reap the rules of the harvest just like everyone else who has been commissioned throughout the Church's history.

Connection:
Rules of Engagement (ROE)

Calling, equipping, commissioning, and releasing has been God's designed process for the advancement and expansion of His Kingdom. We see it in the Old Testament through individuals like Moses, Elijah, Elisha, David, and the prophets. In the New Testament, the Apostle (sent one) to the World, Jesus, was called (Matt. 1.18-23; Heb. 1.2), equipped (Matt. 4.1-11), commissioned (Matt. 3.13-17) and released (Matt. 4.17). He then calls the twelve (Mark 3.13), names them as Apostles (Mark 3.14), equips them (Mark 6.7; Luke 9.1; Acts 1.3), commissions and then releases them into missions (Matt. 28.19 w/Acts 1.8). God's designed process hasn't changed except now He works through appointed leadership in His Church. Paul of Tarsus was the first to go through God's designed process through the appointed leadership of the Church of Antioch.

Three days after his conversion, Paul receives his calling into Apostolic missions from Jesus as communicated through Ananias (Acts 9.15-16). Though we don't know all the details of the next ten to fifteen years of his life, other than he immediately was evangelizing (Acts 9.20 and 28), we can assume that the Spirit of the Lord is equipping Paul for his calling. All that was needed to complete God's designed process was the authorization and releasing through the leadership of a local Church. Barnabas, through the Holy Spirit, goes to Tarsus and brings Paul to the Church in Antioch (Acts 11.24-26a). Though called and equipped, Paul willingly and intentionally submits himself to the appointed godly leadership (elders) of the Antioch Church. They apparently determine he needs some further equipping in teaching (Acts 11.26b) and the stewarding of finances for the relief and care of the suffering and need within the Body of Christ (Acts 11.27-30). He continues this for one year (Acts 11.26b) until the leaders, through the Holy Spirit, authorize and release Paul into his calling as the Apostle to the Gentiles (Acts 13.1-3). With this understanding, here are two critical insights to move forward in Apostolic Missions:

1. We cannot by-pass the local church as God's agent for His designed process for apostolic missions. The smallest of compromises will lead to the slowing, stand still and potentially the ceasing of missions. This is especially important given, that in the West, most do not see the Church as central and pivotal in our culture. The Church is just one, and to many a dying and powerless one, of the systems that make up our culture. Satan has hated the Bride of Christ since her founding. He has masterfully moved her away from being central in this age of the new covenant. He has woven his lie, "who needs the church anyway" and it has stuck. Unfortunately, this lie has stuck to many who profess Jesus. They feel the same way, "I can do without the Church."

    The truth is, for the eight reasons listed above about the Church, she is central to the unseen spiritual world and to the seen world in which we are strangers and aliens. The local church, through Spirit filled leadership, is the only agent in which God works His Kingdom mission. This is the time for the Church to aggressively pray to the

Lord of Harvest to send workers into the harvest field of lost souls. And when He responds, and He will because His desire is that none should perish, then the local church is the only place for these workers to have their calling recognized. It is here that they can be identified, apprenticed, commissioned and released into missions.

2. Another subtle scheme that Satan is focused on is to malign the necessity of submission to authority. He has been at this since before the creation of the world. It was his rebellion to submit to the authority of the Creator God that caused His banishment from Heaven and ultimately to eternal damnation in the Lake of Fire (Rev. 20.10).

In his own pride, arrogance, and un-submissive spirit, He was banished from heaven to earth, and brought this same spirit to our first parents in the Garden of Eden. His half-truth, "Did God say," set into motion a questioning of submission to the Authority of God. And as we know, their rebellion led to their downfall resulting in death, pain, struggle, and sorrow. To this day, the knowledge of good and evil binds us to question authority. To submit to another, whether visible (humanity) or invisible (God), grates against our drive to be like God, i.e., to be our own authority, our own god.

Jesus enters into time and history and lives out what submission to authority looks like as the Son of Man. He was submissive as a child to his earthly father and mother, "And he went down with them and came to Nazareth and was submissive to them" (Luke 2.51a). His ministry starts with submission to John through baptism, "But Jesus answered him, 'Let it be so now, for thus it is fitting for us to fulfill all righteousness" (Matt. 3.15). Jesus's life was unashamedly and perfectly submitted to the will of God the Father, "For I have come down from heaven (sent), not to do my own will but the will of Him who sent me" (John 6.38).

When Jesus taught us to pray, "Thy Kingdom come, Thy will be done" are we not praying for submission to the rule and reign of God and His authority?

The Apostle Paul was steeped into the spirit of submission (Rom. 13.1, 5; Eph. 6.5-9). Insubordination was a disqualifier for one seeking to be an Elder (Titus 1.6b). Submission to authority is little valued in our culture. It, too, has infiltrated the Church. Just look at some social media sites and read comments by professing Christians. Everyone is right in their own eyes and have no need to submit to church authority (good shepherds) because they know good from evil more than their pastors, elders, and spiritual parents and grandparents in the Lord Jesus. If one can't submit to someone they see, how can they submit to someone they can't see? This all-but-forgotten qualification must not be compromised in identifying church planters to apprentice.

Connection Story

In 2005, World Impact leadership, asked me to relocate to South Central with my family and strengthen our church planting efforts in communities of poverty. Being new to Los Angeles, I was praying to the Spirit to lead me to Kingdom leaders within the urban harvest in which to come alongside and partner to further expand and advance God's Kingdom through church planting. In His faithfulness, the Spirit led me to Reverend Hector Cedillo. Hector planted *The Church by the Lake* in MacArthur Park. This unassuming gathering of the homeless, addicts, and forgotten met weekly under a large tree next to the lake. There was no roof but the leaves of the trees and no walls in which to gather. For a season I would load up the folding chairs at the World Impact center and bring them over to the park to set them up for the service. One Sunday we brought a tank, filled it with water, and baptized those who were being saved. Faithfully, the Lord's Supper was administered. The word was preached and worship in praise songs filled the park each Sunday. It was a bona fide Church, a Kingdom Outpost. Together we evangelized, established the Urban Church Association, equipped saints for the work of ministry (2005-2013) when World Impact leadership asked me to relocate to Newark, New Jersey, and give oversite to our mission efforts on the East Coast. In 2015, Dr. Reverend Hank Voss sent me the following update on what the Lord was doing through Hector in equipping many of the "least of these" to advance the Gospel leading to other churches being planted.

> **The Lord does not look at the things man looks at. Man looks at the outward appearance, but the Lord looks on the heart.**
>
> ~ 1 Samuel 16.7b

There is often a divine irony in those leaders God selects. They are those who the world would least expect to be God's special choice. Rev. Hector Cedillo, an inner-city church planter from the mid-Wilshire area of Los Angeles is one clear example. Hector was in his early thirties when he finally decided to turn his life over to Christ, and by that point, he had few options left.

Hector sat in a room looking at his wife. After a five-day binge which almost ended in a drug overdose, his wife and brother had finally found him at a cheap hotel in downtown LA. They brought Hector home, he had wasted all the grocery and rent money during the binge, and now sat weeping, crying like a baby. His wife tenderly asked him, "Hector, you have tried so many things. You have tried alcohol, cocaine, heroin, illegal business, probably even women . . . but why don't you try God? What have you got to lose?"

She was not exaggerating. For years Hector had been heavily involved with alcohol and drugs. He had been homeless and had lived as an addict on the streets. At that time, Hector was selling drugs to support his habit in MacArthur Park, a center for all kinds of crime in downtown Los Angeles. Completely broken, Hector finally listened to his wife, and turned his life over to Christ. From that night on, he was completely freed from alcohol and drugs. He had a new hunger for the Word, showing up to church hours early, and one day read his Bible from 6:00 am until 5:00 pm.

Hector was discipled for two years by a retired missionary, and then began to take classes at a local Bible Institute. One Sunday in the fall of 1999 he returned to Macarthur Park to share his faith with any who would listen. Eventually he met World Impact missionary Ricardo Hong. Ricardo had been prayer walking in that neighborhood for six months looking for the right person to partner with in planting a new church. Immediately a bond was formed, and over the next four years Ricardo and Hector worked together to plant The Church by The Lake, a church where the weekly attendance consists of about fifty percent homeless, alcoholics, and drug addicts.

The Church by the Lake planted its first church in 2004. Hector is believing God for at least 343 (7x7x7) daughter, granddaughter, and great granddaughter churches to be planted before he dies. Hector's disciples [apprentices] and TUMI students have been involved in sixteen church plants.

More than twenty leaders from the Church by the Lake have become TUMI students, and as of the end of 2014, Hector and his TUMI students have seen 16 church plants commissioned in five countries. He sees a whole army of leaders in the men and women around him, individuals who many in our world have given up on. Many of the leaders who are being raised up through his ministry have testimonies similar to his own.

A key component of his strategy to train the many leaders that are emerging is The Urban Ministry Institute (TUMI). The Urban Ministry Institute ensures that all of his leaders, whatever their background, are getting the kind of theological education they need for faithful ministry in the churches they are planting. All of Hector's church planters in training [apprentices] are taking classes at The Urban Ministry Institute. Hector himself has been involved as a mentor at The Urban Ministry Institute and sees TUMI as vital if the church planting movement he is believing God for is going to take place.

Hector's ministry continues to expand. Recently he was on local television asking LA's Mayor about his plans for the homeless in downtown LA. New associations of urban churches are being formed under his leadership in LA County. Besides his local ministry, Hector has preached and done evangelism in many countries including: Mexico, Cuba, Guatemala, France, Italy, Spain, Portugal, and Senegal, Liberia and Sierra Leone. God's choice in leadership selection may surprise us, but he is indeed being glorified through urban leaders like Rev. Hector Cedillo, and the communities of the King which are being planted in America's inner cities.

I catch up with Hector on Facebook and I am thrilled and encouraged to say he is still "moving forward to multiply."

CHAPTER 5

THE KINGDOM: Embrace

Key Old Testament Verse

Yours, O Lord, is the greatness and the power and the glory and the victory and the majesty, for all that is in the heavens and in the earth is yours. Yours is the kingdom, O Lord, and you are exalted as head above all.

~ 1 Chronicles 29.11

Key New Testament Verse

So if there is any encouragement in Christ, any comfort from love, any participation in the Spirit, any affection and sympathy, complete my joy by being of the same mind, having the same love, being in full accord and of one mind.

~ Philippians 2.1-2

Contact: Situation Awareness

Rather than share a personal story I want to share this article from a British atheist named Matthew Parris. He was a writer for the *London Times*. On December 27, 2008 (reposted January 7, 2009 in The Richard Dawkins Foundation's official website) he wrote the following article, "As an atheist, I truly believe Africa needs God."

Before Christmas I returned, after 45 years, to the country that as a boy I knew as Nyasaland. Today it's Malawi, and The Times Christmas Appeal includes a small British charity working there. Pump Aid helps rural communities to install a simple pump, letting people keep their village wells sealed and clean. I went to see this work.

It inspired me, renewing my flagging faith in development charities. But travelling in Malawi refreshed another belief, too: one I've been trying to banish all my life, but an observation I've been unable to avoid since my African childhood. It confounds my ideological beliefs, stubbornly refuses to fit my world view, and has embarrassed my growing belief that there is no God.

Now a confirmed atheist, I've become convinced of the enormous contribution that Christian evangelism makes in Africa: sharply distinct from the work of secular NGOs, government projects and international aid efforts. These alone will not do. Education and training alone will not do. In Africa Christianity changes people's hearts. It brings a spiritual transformation. The rebirth is real. The change is good.

I used to avoid this truth by applauding – as you can – the practical work of mission churches in Africa. It's a pity, I would say, that salvation is part of the package, but Christians black and white, working in Africa, do heal the sick, do teach people to read and write; and only the severest kind of secularist could see a mission hospital or school and say the world would be better without it. I would allow that if faith was needed to motivate missionaries to help, then, fine: but what counted was the help, not the faith.

But this doesn't fit the facts. Faith does more than support the missionary; it is also transferred to his flock. This is the effect that matters so immensely, and which I cannot help observing.

First, then, the observation. We had friends who were missionaries, and as a child I stayed often with them; I also stayed, alone with my little brother, in a traditional rural African village. In the city we had working for us Africans who had converted and were strong believers. The Christians were always different. Far from having cowed or confined its converts, their faith appeared to have liberated and relaxed them. There was a liveliness, a curiosity, an engagement with the world – a directness in their dealings with others – that seemed to be missing in traditional African life. They stood tall.

At 24, travelling by land across the continent reinforced this impression. From Algiers to Niger, Nigeria, Cameroon, and the Central African Republic, then right through the Congo to Rwanda, Tanzania and Kenya, four student friends and I drove our old Land Rover to Nairobi. We slept under the stars, so it was important as we reached the more populated and lawless parts of the sub-Sahara that every day we find somewhere safe by nightfall. Often near a mission.

Whenever we entered a territory worked by missionaries, we had to acknowledge that something changed in the faces of the people we passed and spoke to: something in their eyes, the way they approached you direct, man-to-man, without looking down or away. They had not become more deferential towards strangers – in some ways less so – but more open.

This time in Malawi it was the same. I met no missionaries. You do not encounter missionaries in the lobbies of expensive hotels discussing development strategy documents, as you do with the big NGOs. But instead, I noticed that a handful of the most impressive African members of the Pump Aid team (largely from Zimbabwe) were, privately, strong Christians. "Privately" because the charity is entirely secular, and I never heard any of its team so much as mention religion while working in the villages. But I picked up the Christian references in our conversations.

One, I saw, was studying a devotional textbook in the car. One, on Sunday, went off to church at dawn for a two-hour service.

It would suit me to believe that their honesty, diligence, and optimism in their work were unconnected with personal faith. Their work was secular, but surely affected by what they were. What they were was, in turn, influenced by a conception of man's place in the Universe that Christianity had taught.

There's long been a fashion among Western academic sociologists for placing tribal value systems within a ring fence, beyond critiques founded in our own culture: "theirs" and therefore, best for "them"; authentic and of intrinsically equal worth to ours.

I don't follow this. I observe that tribal belief is no more peaceable than ours; and that it suppresses individuality. People think collectively; first in terms of the community, extended family and tribe. This rural-traditional mindset feeds into the "big man" and gangster politics of the African city: the exaggerated respect for a swaggering leader, and the (literal) inability to understand the whole idea of loyal opposition.

Anxiety – fear of evil spirits, of ancestors, of nature and the wild, of a tribal hierarchy, of quite everyday things – strikes deep into the whole structure of rural African thought. Every man has his place and, call it fear or respect, a great weight grinds down the individual spirit, stunting curiosity. People won't take the initiative, won't take things into their own hands or on their own shoulders.

How can I, as someone with a foot in both camps, explain? When the philosophical tourist moves from one world view to another he finds – at the very moment of passing into the new – that he loses the language to describe the landscape to the old. But let me try an example: the answer given by Sir Edmund Hillary to the question: Why climb the mountain? "Because it's there," he said.

To the rural African mind, this is an explanation of why one would not climb the mountain. It's . . . well, there. Just there. Why interfere? Nothing to be done about it, or with it. Hillary's further explanation - that nobody else had climbed it - would stand as a second reason for passivity.

Christianity, post-Reformation and post-Luther, with its teaching of a direct, personal, two-way link between the individual and God, unmediated by the collective, and insubordinate to any other human being, smashes straight through the philosophical/ spiritual framework I've just described. It offers something to hold on to those anxious to cast off a crushing tribal groupthink. That is why and how it liberates.

Those who want Africa to walk tall amid 21st-century global competition must not kid themselves that providing the material means or even the knowhow that accompanies what we call development will make the change. **A whole belief system must first be supplanted. And I'm afraid it has to be supplanted by another.** *Removing Christian evangelism from the African equation may leave the continent at the mercy of a malign fusion of Nike (materialism*), the witch Doctor (false religion*), the mobile phone (pseudo relationships*) and the machete (anarchy and violence*) (* mine).*

✓ ────── **Content 1:**
✓ ────── **Missions Plank: *The Kingdom***
✓ ────── It takes an atheist to recognize what it takes for
✓ ────── true transformation to happen. Development,
✓ ────── though desperately needed and always in front
of our eyes, is not what will make the change in Africa or anywhere else in the world. Not the inner cities of America or the slums of Delhi. A belief system must be supplanted and replaced by another system and this supplanting must take place in every individual. Matthew Parris, without realizing it, was

communicating what that belief system is. It is the Kingdom of God. Paul the Apostle, through the Holy Spirit, wrote to the Corinthian Church, "Therefore, if anyone is in Christ, he is a new creation. The old has passed away; behold, the new has come" (2 Cor. 5.17).

It's not enough to supplant the old system in an individual. It must be replaced by the Kingdom, i.e., the system of His rule and reign. If not, the situation of the individual may be worse that the original belief system. "When the unclean spirit has gone out of a person, it passes through waterless places seeking rest, and finding none it says, 'I will return to my house from which I came.' And when it comes, it finds the house swept and put in order. Then it goes and brings seven other spirits more evil than itself, and they enter and dwell there. And the last state of that person is worse than the first" (Luke 11.24-26).

That is exactly what Matthew Parris was stating in his last sentence. Removing the evangelism of the Gospel from Africa and just focusing on development, ". . . may leave the continent at the mercy of a malign fusion of Nike (materialism), the witch Doctor (false religion), the mobile phone (pseudo relationships) and the machete (anarchy and violence)." Evil spirits will take over.

The Kingdom of God, His rule and reign, is immediate (Mark 1.15; Luke 17.20-21), progressive (Matt. 13.31-32), and cataclysmic (Matt. 11.12). It is under no threat (Rev. 11.15). The Kingdom of God is inclusive and exclusive. Those who are in the Kingdom have God as their Father (inclusive). God is not the Father of all (exclusive). Paul the Apostle divides humanity into two classes: those "in Christ" and those "not in Christ." God is peculiarly the Father of all who believe, irrespective of nationality, race, gender, age, or class. We are all created in the image of God, but we are not all sons and daughters therefore we are not all brothers and sisters:

And now, little children, abide in him, so that when he appears we may have confidence and not shrink from him in shame at his coming. If you know that he is righteous, you may be sure that everyone who practices righteousness has been born of him.

~ 1 John 2.28-29

By this it is evident who are the children of God, and who are the children of the devil: whoever does not practice righteousness is not of God, nor is the one who does not love his brother.

~ 1 John 3.10

Jesus answered him, "Truly, truly, I say to you, unless one is born again he cannot see the kingdom of God."

~ John 3.3

Jesus said to them, "If God were your Father, you would love me, for I came from God and I am here. I came not of my own accord, but he sent me. Why do you not understand what I say? It is because you cannot bear to hear my word. You are of your father the devil, and your will is to do your father's desires. He was a murderer from the beginning, and does not stand in the truth, because there is no truth in him. When he lies, he speaks out of his own character, for he is a liar and the father of lies."

~ John 8.42-44

The reason why you do not hear them is that you are not of God.

~ John 8.47

. . . in which you once walked, following the course of this world, following the prince of the power of the air, the spirit that is now at work in the sons of disobedience.

~ Ephesians 2.2

The kingdom culture is supra-cultural. It supersedes all cultures because it is supernatural in origin (John 18.36) and destiny (Luke 1.30-33). The purpose of the Kingdom of God is to rule and reign over all things visible and invisible (1 Cor. 15.24) and that includes the souls of each person from past, present and into the future. Everyone will bow to the reign of the rightful King and His Kingdom either willingly and joyfully in this world or in sorrow and regret in the life afterwards (Phil. 2.10-11; Rom. 14.11). Therefore, God desires that every soul would recognize His redemptive reign and rule in the Son in whom He loves by confessing Jesus as Lord and believing He is alive (Rom. 10.9). We are His ambassadors in this ministry of reconciliation to the spiritually lost and blind. Every soul matters. This is the focus of missions.

The action of the Kingdom is to keep moving forward to multiply. The Church must not leave any stone unturned. We must, "Go out into the highways and hedges, and compel them to come in, that my house may be filled" (Luke 14.23). God wants a full house with no quarantines or social distancing. The pandemic of the Kingdom of Darkness is no more. We have the Gospel and therefore we need to advance and expand the Kingdom of God in places where there is no Community of the Kingdom. We must not be like the servant in Luke 19 who buried what was given to him rather than do all he can to multiply his talent. He was condemned for his cowardice. There is no room for cowards in the Kingdom of God. Why? Our five missions planks answer this question: *Jesus is Lord* over all things and there is nothing to fear. We have been entrusted with the power of *the Gospel. The Holy Spirit* has been given to us to comfort and lead us. We, *the Church* are His Bride. What groom will not protect and provide for his beloved. And the righteousness, peace and joy of *the Kingdom* is within the Church. What is there to be cowardly about when standing upon these apostolic missions planks?

The Kingdom of God is the domain of His rule and reign. It quietly and unassumingly entered into the domain of darkness, this present world, which lies in a real, supernatural power (Matt. 4.8-9; 1 John 5.19), the god of this age also known as the prince of the power of the air. Jesus, the rightful King of the Kingdom of God, came preaching God's redemptive rule and reign. "The time is fulfilled, and the kingdom of God is at hand; repent and believe in the gospel." It was the beginning of the conflict and victory over Satan and his kingdom domain of terror, bondage, struggle, and death.

To expand and advance the Kingdom of God is to proclaim the Gospel and call people to repent and believe. It is a call to change one's allegiance. It's a call to "whose side are you on?" Who is ultimately going to rule and reign in the person's life? Whoever relinquishes their self-allegiance, to the authority and redemption of God in Christ Jesus, has found the treasure buried in the ground (Matt. 13.44). The Kingdom of God has entered within (Luke 17.20-21).

Not everyone enters into the Kingdom of God though (Mark 10.14; 23-25; Luke 18.17; Matt. 8.12; Luke 13.28; 1 Cor. 6.9; Gal. 5.21). It is free but there is a cost. Dietrich Bonhoeffer said it best: "Grace is absolutely free, but it will cost you everything." Jesus, the King of God's Kingdom, went about to the cities teaching that "the kingdom of heaven has suffered violence, and the violent take it by force" (Matt. 11.12). God's rule and reign requires a radical reaction. Jesus described this reaction in images of violent action against oneself. "If your hand causes you to sin, cut it off; if your eye causes you to sin, pluck it out" (Mark 9.43, 47). Elsewhere Jesus uses violent language of hating one's family for his sake (Luke 14.26). He said that he did not come to bring peace but a sword (Matt 10.34). The presence of the Kingdom demands a radical reaction (Luke 16.16). This is the inner reaction of what it means to relinquish one's allegiance to the King and His Kingdom. It is self-death (Gal. 2.20).

Whether one submits to the rightful King or not has no effect on the Kingdom. We do not make up the Kingdom. The Kingdom makes and molds us upon entry into it. The message of the Gospel of Jesus Christ that is received by faith through grace, can set free the most rebellious of souls that are trapped and bound in the domain of the dark kingdom and transport that soul into God's Kingdom domain (Col. 1.13). Those who do are brought into the Kingdom society, commit to embracing each other as brothers and sisters in the Family of God.

Content 2:
"E" of an Apostolic Missions Platform:
Embrace

We live on the razors edge of the presence of the Kingdom's righteousness, peace and joy in the Holy Spirit (Rom. 14.17) and the darkness and terror of the Day of the Lord (Joel 2). The apostolic mind is set on the certainty that the Satanic Kingdom of Darkness will be crushed and God's Kingdom will rule over all (Rev. 11.15). It is a mind set on today. Choose you this day whom you will serve (Josh. 24.14-15). This Gospel of the Kingdom must be proclaimed throughout the whole world before the end comes (Matt. 24.14). The vastness of the task demands that we embrace – to take or clasp in the arms; press to the bosom; hug; to take or receive gladly or eagerly; accept willingly – as one Church moving forward in apostolic missions. We must take on the spirit of Gideon and strike as one man (Judg. 6.16).

As we pray for God's Kingdom to come, the Holy Spirit brings His Church together for the common task of missions. We embrace in all our diversity under one banner – The Kingdom of God. We are one body and one Spirit; called to the one hope; one Lord, one faith, one baptism, and one God and Father of all, who is over all and through all and in all (Eph. 4.4-6). The enemy of the rightful King and His Kingdom will do all he can to break the embrace. When the enemy breaks the embrace, and we become segregated, then the enemy has slowed down the "war effort." Missions ceases to move forward. We must not let that happen. We must keep moving forward in solidarity.

When the Church embraces together to combat one enemy for the expansion and advancement of God's Kingdom a spontaneous expansion takes place. "So the churches were strengthened in the faith, and they increased in numbers daily" (Acts 16.5). Though we are scattered on different spiritual war fronts around the world, the Church Militant is one, and is under the direction of the Holy Spirit. We must be the spiritual Allied Forces waging our battles against one spiritual Axis Force. It is critical that the church, local and regional, see themselves as a "resistance location" and not a resort location.

This "E" on the *Apostolic Platform of Missions* must be fought for. The enemy is relentless and ruthless. He has all kinds of resources at his disposal (Matt. 4.8-9). If he attempted to hinder Jesus from his mission (Matt. 16.21-23) he will surely do all in his power to kill our mission efforts. We are stronger together than we are separated. We must be intentional in our efforts to embrace together for missions. The Evangel Network is committed to this for the common effort to keep moving forward to multiply.

Evangel was forged in the fire of a passion for Christ (the Lord), a burden for souls (the Gospel), a love for His Bride (the Church), and confidence in the power of the Holy Spirit (the Holy Spirit) to lead, save, and transform all those who respond and to bring them into the Kingdom of God (the Kingdom). We exist to be a *dynamic catalyst for the health and multiplication of movements*. We embrace all denominations, networks, associations, and local churches who resonate with:

1. Our Purpose – *the Gospel of the Kingdom proclaimed by the empowered urban poor to every people group through indigenous churches and movements*

2. Our Mission – *to empower urban leaders and partner with local churches to reach their city with the Gospel*

3. Our Vision – *a healthy church planted in every community of poverty*

4. Our Theological Confession – *the Word of God as illumined by the Holy Spirit and expressed in the Nicene Creed*

5. Our Strategic Commitments – *evangelism, discipleship, leadership development, church planting, and church planting movements as expressed in World Impact's PLANT acrostic (Prepare, Launch, Assemble, Nurture, Transition)*

6. Our Focus – *to equip church plant trainers working among the poor to run their own Evangel School of Urban Church Planting within their ministry context*

The Kingdom of God is a movement. It is not static but constantly expanding and advancing. It works itself throughout the universe to attain a specific end. What is that end? "Then comes the end, when he delivers the kingdom to God the Father after destroying every rule and every authority and power" (1 Cor. 15.24). Everyone who has submitted to the obedient faith of the Lord Jesus, the rightful King, will be under His loving Kingly reign for all eternity.

Presently we see signs of Kingdom movement in and through the lives of Christ followers who submit to His rule (Acts 4.13). This movement is in their new creation DNA. "And we, who with unveiled faces all reflect the Lord's glory, are being transformed into his likeness with ever-increasing glory, which comes from the Lord, who is the Spirit" (2 Cor. 3.18). Some translations say, "being transformed from glory to glory." There is movement taking place within us as we are being conformed into the image of Christ (Rom. 8.29) with the completion taking place on the Day of Christ (Phil. 1.6).

That Day has not come yet. We only experience a foretaste and not the fullness of the Kingdom. As George Eldon Ladd said, it is the "Not Yet/Already Kingdom." We are to be on our guard and alert because we do not know the time when he will return (Mark 13.33). Standing guard and alert doesn't mean inactivity. We must keep moving forward keeping in step with the Holy Spirit (Gal. 5.25) as He directs His Church in missions. And as we move forward, we must embrace.

Connection:
Rules of Engagement (ROE)

All people naturally seek things. To aimlessly go through life is not how we are created. People need something that gives them worth, meaning, purpose, existence. It makes us who we are. It could be anything from seeking a title like a PhD to aligning oneself with a sports team. Not that these are bad in-and-of themselves but where are they in the priority list of the heart? Are they first? Are you the master dictating to yourself these priorities in your life?

There is only one instance where the Lord Jesus gives His disciples a mandate with an order of priority and a sure reward and that is found in Matthew 6.33, "Seek first the Kingdom of God and His righteousness and all these things will be added unto you." Jesus calls all of humanity to seek and commit to the rule and reign of God in our lives. We are to seek this first. For those who like to set goals of priority then this sums it up. It is nice and neat. It is simple but not simplistic. It will cost you everything yet give you everything. Not only is this our first priority, but once found and we sell everything to obtain the treasure (Matt. 13.44), we are to pray for the rule and reign of God to be here on earth just as it is in heaven (Matt. 6.10).

The Kingdom of God, His rule and reign, is inevitable. Jesus, while walking this earth, knew this reality. Everyone will bow their knee (Phil. 2.10) to the ruler of this Kingdom, Jesus the Lord. And when that time comes, the kingdom of this world and its ruler, the prince of the power of the air, "will become the Kingdom of our Lord of His Christ and He will reign forever and ever" (Rev. 11.15). But that time hasn't come yet. Now is the day of salvation (2 Cor. 6.2) and those who have submitted to the rule and reign of the Kingdom of God, who have found the treasure in the field and sold all they have to purchase it (Matt. 13.44), are tasked to pray and to go and urge others to seek it.

In 2000, Dr. Don Davis, wrote a short manifesto called *Let God Arise: A sober Call to Prevailing Prayer for a Dynamic Spiritual Awakening and the Aggressive Advancement of the Kingdom in America's Inner Cities.* In the manifesto, Dr. Davis writes that a "deep conviction that the cities of the world could not be won without an outpouring of the Holy Spirit on the people of God in the city." If ever this conviction was true, it is now. The cities of the world are going from bad to worse, from evil to evil. What David saw while overlooking his city has been multiplied many times over, "For I see the violence and the strife in the city. Day and night they prowl about on its walls. Destructive forces are at work in the city. Malice and abuse are within it. Threats and lies never leave its streets (Ps. 55.10-11). Destructive forces are at work in the city" (Ps. 55).

We need the Kingdom to come and invade this world. Without the Lord's intervention there is no hope. As Dr. Davis says, "the city would be utterly futile if the Lord failed to 'show up and show out.'" It is only God who can take cities for Himself. Only He can confront the forces of darkness and the spiritual darkness that is woven into all the systems of the nations – education, government, legal, etc. "Only a visitation from the Lord Himself, awakening His people and advancing His Kingdom, could possibly make a difference among so many millions [billions] of people suffering under the tyranny of the enemy. God must arise, scatter His enemies, and demonstrate His power, redeeming souls, transforming lives, and changing urban neighborhoods through a fresh visitation of the Holy Spirit."

In our missions mandate to engage in this spiritual war, our secret will lie in our embracing together in aggressive, sustained prayer. It is our communication piece to listen for our directives from the Spirit of the Lord so that we can move forward according to where He is already convicting of sin and righteousness and judgement (John 16.8). It is also by prayer and supplication with thanksgiving we can make our requests known to God (Phil. 4.6). It is in this embracing that the peace of God which surpasses all understanding guards our hearts and minds in Christ Jesus (Phil. 4.7).

In all our denominational differences, we can embrace in prayer, "Yours, O Lord, is the greatness and the power and the glory and the victory and the majesty, for all that is in the heavens and in the earth is yours. Yours is the kingdom, O Lord, and you are exalted as head above all. Both riches and honor come from you, and you rule over all. In your hand are power and might, and in your hand it is to make great and to give strength to all. And now we thank you, our God, and praise your glorious name" (1 Chron. 29.11-13). We can all unite around the one constant and that is our God is the author, sustainer, and provider for missions. There is no Christian tribe – past-present-future – that does not have this same missions heart of God, and that is to see that none perish but all be reconciled and at peace with God by the blood of his cross (Col. 1.20). He has given us this ministry of reconciliation (2 Cor. 5.18-21). If anyone claims Christ, whether individual or Tribe, and does not have this heart, then they are not of God.

It has been said that the Church moves forward on its knees. Let us embrace and "strike as one" (Judg. 6.16) against the forces of darkness knowing that God will sustain and provide according to His will and purpose in our missions calling to the lost and least of these. Learn more about the, Let God Arise, prayer movement by going to *www.tumi.org/pray*. Seek the Holy Spirit on how He might want you involved in the prayer movement for missions.

Connection Story

I want to share a negative story to bring out the critical importance for the Church to embrace together as one unified force moving forward with the Gospel against one evil spiritual destructive force. There are few times when I wanted to "pack my bags" and turn my back from the call to missions that the Lord Jesus had given me. This is one of those times.

A brutal injustice had taken place in the poor community that Susan and I were bringing up our family. It was an African American community. Racial tensions were high and trust in the police force was low. Being an active member of an alliance of African American churches opened up many doors for me to serve and to have a Kingdom voice in these challenging times. I was the only white person in the alliance but garnished respect because I lived in the community, when even the pastors, whose churches were in the community, would not live here.

One fateful night, an African American man was shot and killed by the police. The neighbors reported that the police had chased the individual, who was the suspect of a crime, into an abandoned home not far from where we lived. It was heard that the man was screaming to, "Get the dogs off me! Get the dogs off me!" Not too long after that, the killing shots were heard. Come to find out, the shots were fired into his back, while he laid sprawled out on the wooden floor, face down. It was an injustice that was the spark to ignite the community in outrage. They demanded justice.

Serving on the Chief of Police's Community Task Force, I began to visit the various community gatherings to listen, and when received, to pray and lend support. One such gathering, was the pastors, elders, leaders from the African American community. A gathering in which I would feel at home with my spiritual family. It was a needed time to embrace as one family and priesthood under the banner of the Lord Jesus.

The church where the gathering took place was not far from where I lived. The parking lot was full. As I walked into the sacred walls of the church, the place was packed and the conversations loud and intense. Over 150 gathered that afternoon. I saw many pastors that I knew and I was looking forward to the time of prayer, discussion, and possible outcomes. It was like being with family, my spiritual family.

As the meeting was getting ready to start, I looked for an open spot to sit in one of the wooden pews. I was the only white brother in the group. Things were beginning to quiet down when two Sergeants-at-Arms walked off the front platform and began to make their way my direction. That's when it became quiet. Everyone, myself included, knew something was up but we didn't know what exactly. The two made their way down the pew behind me, while politely excusing themselves. All of a sudden, I felt a tap on my shoulder. "Reverend Engel?" Turning around, with a look of bewilderment, I said, "Yes?" "We would like for you to quietly leave our assembly as we discuss this injustice done to one of our black brothers." "What?" I replied in disbelief. "This gathering is only for black brothers." "But aren't I a brother in Christ? Don't we serve and pray to the same Lord? I live in this community.

I know many of the pastors and leaders in this place." "Yes, but the leadership here, has requested that you leave." Not wanting to cause a commotion, I rose from my seat, excused myself as I scooted my way past friends and brothers, and was escorted out of the assembly. I slowly walked to my car, trying to process what just happened, and then broke down in tears.

What was a negative experience in my life, one that almost caused me to abandon the task, God used to strengthen the *Apostolic Missions Platform* He was instilling deep into my spirit. If the Kingdom of God is to move forward, the Church must embrace each other as one: one body, one Spirit, one hope, one Lord, one faith, and one baptism (Eph. 4.4-6).

KEEP MOVING FORWARD: Endure

Key Old Testament Verse

The Lord said to Moses, "Why do you cry to me? Tell the people of Israel to go forward. Lift up your staff, and stretch out your hand over the sea and divide it, that the people of Israel may go through the sea on dry ground."

~ Exodus 14.15-16

Key New Testament Verse

Therefore, do not throw away your confidence, which has a great reward. For you have need of endurance, so that when you have done the will of God you may receive what is promised. For,

> "Yet a little while,
> and the coming one will come and will not delay;
> but my righteous one shall live by faith,
> and if he shrinks back,
> my soul has no pleasure in him."

But we are not of those who shrink back and are destroyed, but of those who have faith and preserve their souls.

~ Hebrews 10.35-39

From Genesis to Revelation the Bible attributes one determination of God and that is to save humanity. In all of God's dealings with human beings His objective is to populate His Kingdom in the world to come. He is throwing a banquet like none other, and He wants it filled to capacity (Luke 14.16-24). It is going to be the ultimate of celebrations. Until then, we have been called and enlisted to go and proclaim Good News of entry into God's eternal Kingdom and Banquet celebration to all who would submit and believe on the Lord Jesus Christ. We must keep moving forward and not shrink back. We are it and we must not abandon the mission. Now is the time to heed the words of J. Oswald Sanders when he said, "A great deal more failure is the result of an excess of caution than of bold experimentation with new ideas. The frontiers of the Kingdom of God were never advanced by men and women of caution." Excess caution must be stricken from our vocabulary and bold experimentation must be highlighted and applauded in these challenging days in which we live. This was exactly how the Apostle Paul lived and what the early church expected.

The first missionary journey was a bold step of the Antioch Church to advance the Kingdom of God into new frontiers. All caution was thrown into the wind as the send-off team of Paul and Barnabas were commissioned and released (Acts 13.5) to proclaim the Gospel leading them to establish new outposts of the Kingdom wherever the Spirit of the Lord would lead them. John Mark was part of this team but not long into their missions journey, Luke records this short comment in Acts 13.13b, "And John left them and returned to Jerusalem."

Luke does not tell us why John Mark left the missions team and returned to Jerusalem. What we do know is that it was of great importance to the Apostle Paul to the extent that it caused a severe confrontation and break between Paul and Barnabas as they made plans for their second missions journey. To Paul, John Mark's withdrawal (Acts 15.38) was an abandonment, a

desertion from the task they had been commissioned by the
Holy Spirit through the Church leadership in Antioch. Through
prayer, fasting, and the laying on of hands they were released
to expand and advance God's Kingdom into new frontiers.
Faithfulness to the completion of the mission was expected no
matter the cost.

The words of Solomon were etched into Paul's spirit when it came
to spiritual warfare, "There is no discharge from war" (Eccles. 8.8b).
The Apostle Paul new what missions had cost him, "Five times
I received at the hands of the Jews the forty lashes less one. Three
times I was beaten with rods. Once I was stoned. Three times I
was shipwrecked; a night and a day I was adrift at sea; on frequent
journeys, in danger from rivers, danger from robbers, danger
from my own people, danger from Gentiles, danger in the city,
danger in the wilderness, danger at sea, danger from false
brothers; in toil and hardship, through many a sleepless night,
in hunger and thirst, often without food, in cold and exposure.
And, apart from other things, there is the daily pressure on me
of my anxiety for all the churches. Who is weak, and I am not
weak? Who is made to fall, and I am not indignant?" (2 Cor.
11.24-29).

Paul despaired of life (2 Cor. 1.18). Paul knew the cost and it
ultimately cost him his life through martyrdom. How is it that
he could say, "We are afflicted in every way, but not crushed;
perplexed, but not driven to despair; persecuted, but not forsaken;
struck down, but not destroyed" (2 Cor. 4.8-9)? What was it
that kept Paul moving forward when John Mark abandoned the
missions task?

There was something deep in the core of Paul that allowed him
to not shrink back but to press forward in missions. Though
assaulted in every way he did not abandon his calling. He fulfilled/
completed the missions task given to him by proclaiming the
Gospel, making disciples of converts, appointing elders, and

commending them to the Holy Spirit to lead fully functioning churches for the glory of God. What allowed the Apostle to the Gentiles to engage courageously and faithfully in missions? I believe Paul was anchored securely in the Five Planks of Missions. Let's take one last look at these from Acts, the book on missions, and see how each of these planks was firmly established in Paul's platform of missions.

1. *Jesus Is Lord.* "And when we had all fallen to the ground, I heard a voice saying to me in the Hebrew language, 'Saul, Saul, why are you persecuting me? It is hard for you to kick against the goads.' And I said, 'Who are you, Lord?' And the Lord said, 'I am Jesus whom you are persecuting. But rise and stand upon your feet, for I have appeared to you for this purpose, to appoint you as a servant and witness to the things in which you have seen me and to those in which I will appear to you" (Acts 26.14-16).

   The Apostle Paul was forever changed by the Lord Jesus that inevitable day he journeyed to Damascus. Jesus as Lord of all, infiltrated every crevice of his life and it showed in his missionary journeys and in his writings to the Churches he had planted. "For from him and through him and to him are all things. To him be glory forever. Amen" (Rom. 11.36). Jesus is it! It's all about Him. God's purpose, His rule and reign, is focused on Jesus. His death and resurrection secured His Lordship over the kingdoms of this world and the prince of the power of the air (Eph. 2.1-7).

   > For in Him all the fullness of God was pleased to dwell, and through Him to reconcile to Himself all things, whether on earth or in heaven, making peace by the blood of His cross.
   >
   > ~ Colossians 1.19-20

> For by Him all things were created, in heaven and on earth, visible and invisible, whether thrones or dominions or rulers or authorities – all things were created through Him and for Him. And He is before all things, and in Him all things hold together.
>
> ~ Colossians 1.16-17

If Jesus is not Lord, there is no Gospel for He is the Gospel (Rom. 1.16; 2 Cor. 5.18-19; Rom. 5.1). Without Jesus being Lord, there is no Holy Spirit for the Father to send in His name (John 14.26). Without Jesus as Lord overall, there is no Church, for He is the architect and builder of the Church (Matt. 16.18). And without Jesus as Lord, there is no Kingdom for every kingdom must have a Lord, a ruler, and of God's Kingdom that person is Jesus (Rev. 11.15). The foundation on which Evangel's missions-critical Planks rests is the Lordship of Jesus. The Apostle Paul humbly submitted, unashamedly exalted, totally sacrificed and passionately worshiped the Lord Jesus to whom he was endeared to. He knew that apart from Him he could do nothing (John 15.5).

2. *The Holy Spirit.* "While they were worshiping the Lord and fasting, the Holy Spirit said, 'Set apart for me Barnabas and Saul for the work to which I have called them'" (Acts 13.2)

The expansion and advancement of God's Kingdom can only take place through men and women who are called, surrendered, and filled with the Holy Spirit (Acts). He empowers for missions (Acts 1.8), gives directions in missions (Acts 16.6-7), grants divine boldness for witness (Acts 4.13, 31). The Holy Spirit is the Lord, the giver of life, who proceeds from the Father and the Son, and with the Father and the Son is worshipped and glorified (Nicene Creed). The Apostle Paul totally surrendered his life to the third person of the Trinity in order to engage in aggressive missions for Gods Kingdom advancement leading to explosive multiplication and the formation, equipping and strengthening of church planting movements.

3. *The Gospel.* "And he reasoned in the synagogue every Sabbath, and tried to persuade Jews and Greeks. When Silas and Timothy arrived from Macedonia, Paul was occupied with the word, testifying to the Jews that the Christ was Jesus" (Acts 18.4-5).

   There is only one power that causes demons to flee (Mark 1.21-28) and the Kingdom of Darkness to tremble (James 2.19) and that is the Gospel of Jesus Christ. It is the only power of God (Rom. 1.16; 1 Cor. 1.18, 24) in which God is appeased (Rom. 3.21-26) and we now can experience God's peace (Rom. 5.1). To the Apostle Paul it was not the Gospel plus anything else. It is the Gospel and Gospel alone in which rebellious humanity can be reconciled to God (2 Cor. 5.18-19). This is the good news. This is the Gospel. Paul aggressively evangelized lost souls with the only power that will rescue, redeem, reconcile, and restore, and that was with the Gospel of Jesus Christ.

4. *The Church.* "Pay careful attention to yourselves and to all the flock, in which the Holy Spirit has made you overseers, to care for the church of God, which he obtained with his own blood" (Acts 20.28).

   There is nothing in this world like a local Church. To the Church has been given the keys of the Kingdom in which to bind and to lose in the spiritual realm (Matt. 16.19). A small church in a community that is devastated by violence and strife, malice and abuse, threats and lies, demonic destructive forces (Ps. 55.9-11) is an outpost of the Kingdom of God bringing salvation and hope in this world and in the world to come. The planting of a healthy reproducing church in enemy occupied territory is the end task of missions, for the Church is the end game in town. Paul deeply held this conviction, knowing that the church is the agent of the Kingdom where empowerment to multiply healthy, reproducing churches is facilitated.

5. *The Kingdom.* "He [Paul] lived there two whole years at his own expense, and welcomed all who came to him, proclaiming the kingdom of God and teaching about the Lord Jesus Christ with all boldness and without hindrance" (Acts 28.30-31).

The Kingdom of God, His rule and reign, has entered into the world and is expanding and advancing (Matt. 13.31) and the gates of hell cannot stop its movement (Matt. 16.18). The Lord Jesus came preaching the Kingdom of God (Mark 1.15), declaring Himself having the authority (Matt. 28.19), and the one-and-only divine Ruler of the Kingdom of God which is not of this world (John 18.36). As the rightful Ruler, the Lord Jesus is working even now, "destroying (a verb; not complete yet) every rule, and every authority and power" (1 Cor. 15.24). When all His enemies are "under his feet" and "the last enemy to be destroyed is death," then comes the end and the Lord Jesus will deliver the Kingdom to God the Father Almighty (1 Cor. 15.24-26). Paul the Apostle was burdened to see the Church embrace as one "allied force" to expand and advance the Kingdom of God with the proclamation of Good News leading to churches being planted to show visibly what the "Rule of God" looks like when it is embraced by people who acknowledge Christ's lordship.

These five apostolic missions planks were securely "nailed" together in Paul's life, giving him an *Apostolic Missions Platform* in which to move forward and multiply. Standing on this platform gave Paul an eternal perspective to look at the things that are unseen; the really real (2 Cor. 4.15-18). Without these planks being anchored firmly together, the platform becomes unstable. Standing on an unstable platform will cause anyone to shrink back, abandon, withdraw, and to give up. When this happens, one becomes a "John Mark." When the planks of the *Apostolic Missions Platform* are anchored securely we can endure and move forward when we are assaulted from within and without by our spiritual enemy. This does not guarantee churches and church planting movements will happen. Our responsibility is to align ourselves with these apostolic Pauline missions planks so that we can engage in an aggressive *Apostolic Missions Platform*. The growth and movement are always the Lords (1 Cor. 3.6-7).

The feeling to abandon missions is normal, and for good reasons. Missions is waging war "against the rulers, against the authorities, against the cosmic powers over this present darkness, against the spiritual forces of evil in the heavenly places" (Eph. 6.12). The Church battles against an ancient enemy whose intent is not just to squelch the advancement and expansion of the Kingdom of God but to annihilate the Church and its ambassadors.

The enemy comes at us from every front using the various weapons of temptations, trials, pains, struggles, fears, and death. He knows no rules of engagement. He will ruthlessly attack heart, soul, strength, and mind. He will do all he can to put the spirit of cowardice within the bravest of us. But there is no room in the Kingdom of God for cowards (Rev. 21.7-8a). His demonic minions will assault your family and friends. And when you have a slight reprieve from the battle, he will come at you again at an opportune time (Luke 4.13). The "spirit of John Mark" will scream within the Church to abandon the missions mandate. So, what has kept the Church ever pressing forward?

The epigraph for this booklet, *Mere Missions: Moving Forward to Multiply*, is ". . . not of those who shrink back." I sign all my emails with this short quotation from Hebrews 10. I do not do it for the recipient of my email. I do it for me. The temptation to shrink back is there. To abandon missions is a confrontation I have faced many times and expect to face until I depart this spiritual "war zone" that is occupied and led by the prince of the power of the air (Eph. 2.2). This little discipline reminds me to, "destroy arguments and every lofty opinion raised against the knowledge of God and take every thought captive to obey Christ" (2 Cor. 10.5). It strengthens me to stand; to keep moving forward; to endure. It's taken from a longer passage found in Hebrews 10.35-39:

> Therefore, do not throw away your confidence, which has a great reward. For you have need of endurance, so that when you have done the will of God you may receive what is promised. For,
>
>> "Yet a little while,
>> and the coming one will come and will not delay;
>> but my righteous one shall live by faith,
>> and if he shrinks back,
>> my soul has no pleasure in him."
>
> But we are not of those who shrink back and are destroyed, but of those who have faith and preserve their souls.

According to these verses, we apparently have an option. If we are admonished to "not throw away" then it must mean, we can "throw away." The throwing away or keeping is an action on our part. But what is it that we are not to throw away? What are we not to abandon? It is our confidence. And what is our confidence? "The coming one will come and not delay." This is our hope. We are not to abandon our hope for "hope that is seen is not hope.

For who hopes for what he sees? But if we hope for what we do not see, we wait for it with patience" (Rom. 8.24-25).

This is why hope is one of the three theological virtues that Paul mentions to the Corinthian Church (1 Cor. 13.13). Just like any virtue, it is a behavior that we can work at. It becomes an act of the will on our part. It is not enough just to maintain this virtue. We can and must grow stronger, purer, and clearer in our hope. This is not to escape the world. The more we think and hope of the world to come, the more engaged we become in this world. The old phrase, "You're so heavenly minded that you're no earthly good" is the subtle lie of the enemy. The kingdom phrase is "You're so heavenly minded that you are earthly good." The Apostle Paul gives a clear word on this to the Saints in Colossae, "If then you have been raised with Christ, seek the things that are above, where Christ is, seated at the right hand of God. Set your minds on things that are above, not on things that are on earth. For you have died, and your life is hidden with Christ in God. When Christ who is your life appears, then you also will appear with him in glory" (Col. 3.1-4). No matter what comes through the doors of life, we must stand, not shrink back, and move forward in our hope. The rightful King will return. He who promised this cannot lie. He is Lord. We need to endure with patience the battle and not shrink back but move forward in missions.

The early Church was not aware of this escapist teaching. Instead, it taught the biblical doctrine of Christ's Lordship, "Ruler of the kings of the earth." They saw clearly what was written on His robe and on His thigh, "For He has this name written, 'King of kings' and 'Lord of lords.'" It was this that guaranteed their persecution, torture, and death at the hands of the State. And it was also this that guaranteed their ultimate victory. Because Jesus is universal Lord, all opposition to His rule is doomed to failure, and will be crushed. Because Christ is King of kings and Lord of lords, Christians are assured of two things: warfare to the death against all would-be-gods; and the complete triumph of the Christian faith over all its enemies (Rev. 19.15)

The object of all of God's dealings with human beings is "the world to come" (Heb. 2.5). The Day of the Lord that is drawing near. Christ "will appear a second time, not to deal with sin but to save those who are eagerly waiting for him" (Heb. 9.28). We will receive the promised salvation (Heb. 10.36), the rest that remains (Heb. 4.9), the promised homeland (Heb. 11.14), a better country (Heb. 11.16) at His second coming. "For yet a little while and the coming one shall come and shall not tarry" (Heb. 10.37). This age will end with a cosmic catastrophe by which the present world order will be shaken (1.11-12; 13.26) and the true eternal Kingdom of God, now invisible, will become visible. We must hold fast our confidence and pride in our hope (Heb. 10.35).

Again, I quote C. S. Lewis in his book, *Mere Christianity*. In his short but powerful section on hope he says, "I must keep alive in myself the desire for my true country, which I shall not find till after death; I must never let it get snowed under or turned aside; I must make it the main object of life to press on to that other country and to help others to do the same." Fundamentally as Christians we "must keep alive," "must never turn aside," and "must make it the main object of life to press on." We must endure. We must keep moving forward and help others to do the same.

And if we endure, we will reach the goal of our redemption. When Christ's redeeming mission is completed, the greatest of all blessings will be bestowed upon us. We will see God's face (Rev. 22.4). We will live "happily ever after" in God's Kingdom of righteousness, peace and joy with God dwelling in the midst of his people. This is the goal of the long course of redemptive history. *Soli Deo Gloria.*

I conclude my booklet from a short scene from the movie (and book) by J. R. R. Tolkien. Tolkien was an English writer, poet, philologist, and academic, who convinced C. S. Lewis to return to the faith. He is best known as the author of the epic high fantasy works, *The Hobbit* and *The Lord of the Rings*. For those who know me, it would be uncharacteristic for me to not choose a scene from *The Lord of the Rings*, as I am a big fan of the movies. If you haven't read or seen the trilogy, *The Lord of the Rings*, the scene will speak for itself. It would be worth your time though to watch the movies or read the book. Kingdom principles are woven throughout this gripping fantasy.

Samwise Gamgee (Sam) and Frodo Baggins (Mr. Frodo), two hobbits, are confronted with the reality of life, evil, confusion, and their mission. The "John Mark" syndrome is creeping up within them. They don't think they can move forward anymore. It may be time to shrink back and abandon the task. They are losing hope. It is dimming before their eyes. Then Sam understands. He remembers a plank to strengthen their platform so they can stand and keep moving forward. The conversation takes place in the second of three volumes, *The Two Towers*.

Frodo: I can't do this Sam.

Sam: I know. It's all wrong. By rights we shouldn't even be here. But we are. It's like in the great stories, Mr. Frodo. The ones that really mattered. Full of darkness and danger, they were. And sometimes you didn't want to know the end. Because how could the end be happy? How could the world go back to the way it was when so much bad had happened? But in the end, it's only a passing thing, this shadow. Even darkness must pass. A new day will come. And when the sun shines it will shine out the clearer. Those were the stories that stayed with you. That meant something, even if you were too small to understand why. But I think, Mr. Frodo, I do understand. I know now. Folk in those stories had lots of chances of turning back, only they didn't. They kept going. Because they were holding on to something.

Frodo: What are we holding on to Sam?

Sam: That there's some good in this world, Mr. Frodo . . . and it's worth fighting for.

God created the world and saw that it was good. Though the cancer of sin entered the world, God's very nature caused Him to demonstrate His love that, even in the very state of our own rebellion, He sent and sacrificed His only Son to redeem us. The rebels who believe in the liberating work God did in Jesus Christ, enter into the Kingdom Society and participate in a campaign of sabotage. The campaign is brutal. Lives have and will continue to be sacrificed for the Kingdom. We must endure in our evangelism, equipping, and embracing. We must endure in daily submission to the Holy Spirit for His empowerment for missions. And most of all we must endure in our endearment to Jesus for apart from Him there is no way, no truth, and no life. "If we endure, we will also reign with him" (2 Tim. 2.12a).

Sometimes moving forward is not letting go. It is all we can do to hold on. We cry out to the God the gripping words of Jacob, "I will not let you go unless you bless me" (Gen. 32.26). Holding on to the King and His Kingdom automatically moves you forward for the Kingdom of God is movement. It is expanding and advancing apart from us. It's like holding onto a log and letting the current take you. You just need to hold on.

Our hope is sure (Matt. 10.22). The rightful King will come and not delay. Our times demand complete devotion to The Lord Jesus, boldness in the proclamation of The Gospel, absolute surrender and unreserved obedience to The Holy Spirit, deep love and fidelity to The Church, and unflinching loyalty to the Kingdom. Our Missions Platform is anchored on these five

Planks of Missions: Jesus Is Lord. The Gospel. The Holy Spirit. The Church. The Kingdom. This is mere missions. We clearly hear the battle cry, "KEEP MOVING FORWARD AND MULTIPLY."

". . . not of those who shrink back . . ." Hebrews 10.39

Bob

APPENDIX

APPENDIX 1
Ten Church Plant Guiding Principles
World Impact

1	Jesus is Lord.	Matthew 9.37-38
2	Evangelize, Equip, and Empower unreached people to reach people.	1 Thessalonians 1.6-8
3	Be inclusive: Whosoever will may come.	Romans 10.12
4	Be culturally neutral: Come just as you are.	Colossians 3.11
5	Avoid a fortress mentality.	Acts 1.8
6	Continue to evangelize to avoid stagnation.	Romans 1.16-17
7	Cross ethnic, class, gender, and language barriers.	1 Corinthians 9.19-22
8	Respect the dominance of the receiving culture.	Acts 15.23-29
9	Avoid dependence.	Ephesians 4.11-16
10	Think reproducibility.	2 Timothy 2.2; Philippians 1.18

Advancing the Kingdom in the City: Multiplying Congregations with a Common Identity

Rev. Dr. Don L. Davis. *Winning the World: Facilitating Urban Church Planting Movements. Foundations for Ministry Series.* Wichita: The Urban Ministry Institute, 2007.

Acts 2.41-47 (ESV) – So those who received his word were baptized, and there were added that day about three thousand souls. [42] And they devoted themselves to the apostles' teaching and fellowship, to the breaking of bread and the prayers. [43] And awe came upon every soul, and many wonders and signs were being done through the apostles. [44] And all who believed were together and had all things in common. [45] And they were selling their possessions and belongings and distributing the proceeds to all, as any had need. [46] And day by day, attending the temple together and breaking bread in their homes, they received their food with glad and generous hearts, [47] praising God and having favor with all the people. And the Lord added to their number day by day those who were being saved.

koinonia (pronunciation: [koy-nohn-ee'-ah])

Trinitarian Principle: Unity • Diversity • Equality

World Impact seeks to plant churches that are kingdom-oriented communities where Christ is exalted as Lord and the Kingdom of God is advanced in every facet of community life, and, we seek to do this in a way that respects and acknowledges the validity and significance of incarnating this community life in the receiving culture. In order to ensure the viability, protection, and flourishing of these congregations, we ought to explore forming close-knit associations between congregations where a common identity, confession, and faith are practiced, under a common oversight and governance, that connects in a fundamental way the resources and visions of each church without lording over them.

Following is a chart that sketches what might be the elements of such a common coalition of churches which would link their lives in a strategic way for the well-being and enrichment of the entire fellowship of churches. (Cf. *Imagining a Unified, Connected C1 Church Planting Movement* [see *www.tumi.org/Capstone* under the header *Appendices*] which in a comprehensive way suggests what may be included along ecclesial and missional, liturgical, and catechetical lines in such a fellowship).

Sharing a Common Identity, Purpose, and Mission	
A Common Name and Association	Understanding the churches as fundamentally linked in history, identity, legacy, and destiny
A Common Confession of Faith	Developing a common theological and doctrinal vision
A Common Celebration and Worship	Practicing a common liturgy with shared worship approaches
A Common Discipleship and Catechism	Sharing a common curriculum and process for welcoming, incorporating, and discipling new believers into our fellowship
A Common Governance and Oversight	Answering to a common accountability for leadership and care
A Common Service and Missionary Outreach	Developing integrated processes and programs of justice, good works, outreach, evangelism, and missions, both at home and throughout the world
A Common Stewardship and Partnership	Combining resources through consistent mutual contribution to maximize impact for the entire association

Benefits of a Common Movement

1. Sense of belonging through a shared faith and identity

2. Efficiency and economy of effort

3. Ability to plant multiple plants in many different venues and populations

4. Cultivating genuine unity and diversity, with a spirit of mutuality and equality among the congregations

5. Increased productivity and viability within our missions efforts and churches

6. Interchangability and cross pollination

7. Ongoing support and encouragement of our leaders

8. Provide leverage for new projects and new initiatives

9. Standardized processes and procedures for incorporation and training

10. Greater opportunities for convocation and exposure to other like-minded believers

11. Exploration of new connections with other associations with similar vision

12. Assistance in jump starting WI RMO spirituality and unity

APPENDIX 3

Christus Victor:
An Integrated Vision for the Christian Life

Rev. Dr. Don L. Davis

For the Church

- The Church Is the primary extension of Jesus in the world
- Ransomed treasure of the victorious, risen Christ
- *Laos:* The people of God
- God's new creation: presence of the future
- Locus and agent of the Already/Not Yet Kingdom

For Theology and Doctrine

- The authoritative Word of Christ's victory: the Apostolic Tradition: the Holy Scriptures
- Theology as commentary on the grand narrative of God
- *Christus Victor* as core theological framework for meaning in the world
- The Nicene Creed: the Story of God's triumphant grace

For Spirituality

- The Holy Spirit's presence and power in the midst of God's people
- Sharing in the disciplines of the Spirit
- Gatherings, lectionary, liturgy, and our observances in the Church Year
- Living the life of the risen Christ in the rhythm of our ordinary lives

Christus Victor

Destroyer of Evil and Death
Restorer of Creation
Victor o'er Hades and Sin
Crusher of Satan

For Gifts

- God's gracious endowments and benefits from *Christus Victor*
- Pastoral offices to the Church
- The Holy Spirit's sovereign dispensing of the gifts
- Stewardship: divine, diverse gifts for the common good

For Worship

- People of the Resurrection: unending celebration of the people of God
- Remembering, participating in the Christ event in our worship
- Listen and respond to the Word
- Transformed at the Table, the Lord's Supper
- The presence of the Father through the Son in the Spirit

For Evangelism and Mission

- Evangelism as unashamed declaration and demonstration of *Christus Victor* to the world
- The Gospel as Good News of kingdom pledge
- We proclaim God's Kingdom come in the person of Jesus of Nazareth
- The Great Commission: go to all people groups making disciples of Christ and his Kingdom
- Proclaiming Christ as Lord and Messiah

For Justice and Compassion

- The gracious and generous expressions of Jesus through the Church
- The Church displays the very life of the Kingdom
- The Church demonstrates the very life of the Kingdom of heaven right here and now
- Having freely received, we freely give (no sense of merit or pride)
- Justice as tangible evidence of the Kingdom come

APPENDIX 4

The Church Leadership Paradigm:
The Case for Biblical Leadership

Rev. Dr. Don L. Davis

1. The *Kingdom of God* has come in the person of *Jesus of Nazareth*, and is now manifest through the Spirit in the Church.

2. The cities of the world, as strongholds of the devil, desperately need the *presence* and *witness* of the Church.

3. The Church cannot thrive and provide witness without *leadership*.

4. Authentic leadership in the Church must be *called by God, represent Jesus Christ, be gifted by the Spirit, and confirmed by others* in the body.

5. Called, endowed, and confirmed leaders must be given *authority, resources, and opportunity* in order to facilitate maturity and equip the saints for ministry.

Appendix 5

Interaction of Class, Culture, and Race

World Impact

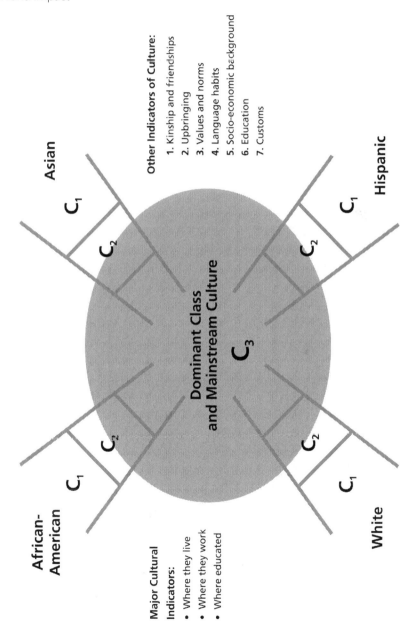

Other Indicators of Culture:

1. Kinship and friendships
2. Upbringing
3. Values and norms
4. Language habits
5. Socio-economic background
6. Education
7. Customs

Asian

C_1

C_2

Hispanic

C_1

C_2

Dominant Class and Mainstream Culture

C_3

C_2

C_2

African-American

C_1

White

C_1

Major Cultural Indicators:

- Where they live
- Where they work
- Where educated

APPENDIX 6
Discipleship Diagram
Rev. Dr. Don L. Davis

2 Timothy 2.2 (ESV) – And what you have heard from me in the presence of many witnesses entrust to faithful men who will be able to teach others also.

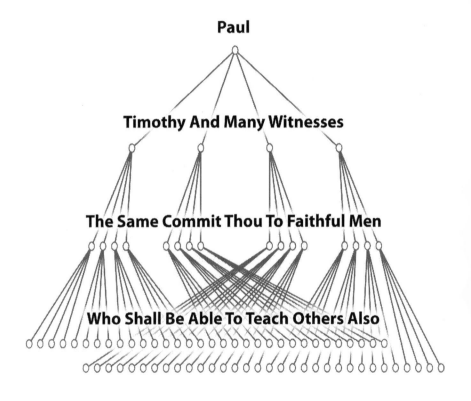

Appendix 7

Discipling the Faithful:
Establishing Leaders for the Urban Church

Rev. Dr. Don L. Davis

	Commission	Character	Competence	Community
Definition	Recognizes the call of God and replies with prompt obedience to his lordship and leading	Reflects the character of Christ in his/her personal convictions, conduct, and lifestyle	Responds in the power of the Spirit with excellence in carrying out their appointed tasks and ministry	Regards multiplying disciples in the body of Christ as the primary role of ministry
Key Scripture	2 Tim. 1.6-14; 1 Tim. 4.14; Acts 1.8; Matt. 28.18-20	John 15.4-5; 2 Tim. 2.2; 1 Cor. 4.2; Gal. 5.16-23	2 Tim. 2.15; 3.16-17; Rom. 15.14; 1 Cor. 12	Eph. 4.9-15; 1 Cor. 12.1-27
Critical Concept	The Authority of **God:** God's leader acts on God's recognized call and authority, acknowledged by the saints and God's leaders	The Humility of **Christ:** God's leader demonstrates the mind and lifestyle of Christ in his or her actions and relationships	The Power of the **Spirit:** God's leader operates in the gifting and anointing of the Holy Spirit	The Growth of the **Church:** God's leader uses all of his or her resources to equip and empower the body of Christ for his/her goal and task
Central Elements	A clear call from God / Authentic testimony before God and others / Deep sense of personal conviction based on Scripture / Personal burden for a particular task or people / Confirmation by leaders and the body	Passion for Christlikeness / Radical lifestyle for the Kingdom / Serious pursuit of holiness / Discipline in the personal life / Fulfills role-relationships and bond-slave of Jesus Christ / Provides an attractive model for others in their conduct, speech, and lifestyle (the fruit of the Spirit)	Endowments and gifts from the Spirit / Sound discipling from an able mentor / Skill in the spiritual disciplines / Ability in the Word / Able to evangelize, follow up, and disciple new converts / Strategic in the use of resources and people to accomplish God's task	Genuine love for and desire to serve God's people / Disciples faithful individuals / Facilitates growth in small groups / Pastors and equips believers in the congregation / Nurtures associations and networks among Christians and churches / Advances new movements among God's people locally
Satanic Strategy to Abort	Operates on the basis of personality or position rather than on God's appointed call and ongoing authority	Substitutes ministry activity and/or hard work and industry for godliness and Christlikeness	Functions on natural gifting and personal ingenuity rather than on the Spirit's leading and gifting	Exalts tasks and activities above equipping the saints and developing Christian community
Key Steps	Identify God's call / Discover your burden / Be confirmed by leaders	Abide in Christ / Discipline for godliness / Pursue holiness in all	Discover the Spirit's gifts / Receive excellent training / Hone your performance	Embrace God's Church / Learn leadership's contexts / Equip concentrically
Results	Deep confidence in God arising from God's call	Powerful Christlike example provided for others to follow	Dynamic working of the Holy Spirit	Multiplying disciples in the Church

APPENDIX 8

Fit to Represent:
Multiplying Disciples of the Kingdom of God

Rev. Dr. Don L. Davis

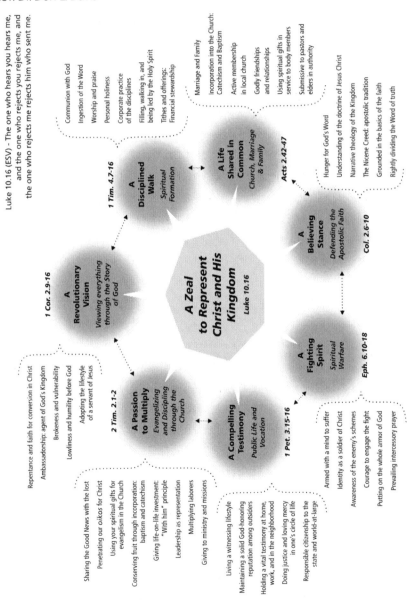

Luke 10.16 (ESV) - The one who hears you hears me, and the one who rejects you rejects me, and the one who rejects me rejects him who sent me.

A Disciplined Walk — *Spiritual Formation* — *1 Tim. 4.7-16*
- Communion with God
- Ingestion of the Word
- Worship and praise
- Personal holiness
- Corporate practice of the disciplines
- Filling, walking in, and being led by the Holy Spirit
- Tithes and offerings: Financial stewardship

A Life Shared in Common — *Church, Marriage & Family* — *Acts 2.42-47*
- Marriage and Family
- Incorporation into the Church: Catechism and Baptism
- Active membership in local church
- Godly friendships and relationships
- Using spiritual gifts in service to body members
- Submissive to pastors and elders in authority

A Believing Stance — *Defending the Apostolic Faith* — *Col. 2.6-10*
- Hunger for God's Word
- Understanding of the doctrine of Jesus Christ
- Narrative theology of the Kingdom
- The Nicene Creed: apostolic tradition
- Grounded in the basics of the faith
- Rightly dividing the Word of truth

A Revolutionary Vision — *Viewing everything through the Story of God* — *1 Cor. 2.9-16*

A Zeal to Represent Christ and His Kingdom — *Luke 10.16*

A Fighting Spirit — *Spiritual Warfare* — *Eph. 6.10-18*
- Armed with a mind to suffer
- Identity as a soldier of Christ
- Awareness of the enemy's schemes
- Courage to engage the fight
- Putting on the whole armor of God
- Prevailing intercessory prayer

A Passion to Multiply — *Evangelizing and Discipling through the Church* — *2 Tim. 2.1-2*
- Repentance and faith for conversion in Christ
- Ambassadorship: agent of God's Kingdom
- Brokeness and vulnerability
- Lowliness and humility before God
- Adopting the lifestyle of a servant of Jesus
- Sharing the Good News with the lost
- Penetrating our *oikos* for Christ
- Using your spiritual gifts for evangelism in the Church
- Conserving fruit through incorporation: baptism and catechism
- Giving life-on-life investment: "With him" principle
- Leadership as representation
- Multiplying laborers
- Giving to ministry and missions

A Compelling Testimony — *Public Life and Vocation* — *1 Pet. 3.15-16*
- Living a witnessing lifestyle
- Maintaining a solid God-honoring reputation among outsiders
- Holding a vital testimony at home, work, and in the neighborhood
- Doing justice and loving mercy in one's circle of life
- Responsible citizenship to the state and world-at-large

APPENDIX 9

From Before to Beyond Time:
The Plan of God and Human History

Adapted from Suzanne de Dietrich. *God's Unfolding Purpose*. Philadelphia: Westminster Press, 1976.

I. Before Time (Eternity Past)

1 Cor. 2.7 (ESV) – But we impart a secret and hidden wisdom of God, which God decreed before the ages for our glory (cf. Titus 1.2).

A. The Eternal Triune God
B. God's Eternal Purpose
C. The Mystery of Iniquity
D. The Principalities and Powers

II. Beginning of Time (Creation and Fall)

Gen. 1.1 (ESV) – In the beginning, God created the heavens and the earth.

A. Creative Word
B. Humanity
C. Fall
D. Reign of Death and First Signs of Grace

III. Unfolding of Time (God's Plan Revealed through Israel)

Gal. 3.8 (ESV) – And the Scripture, foreseeing that God would justify the Gentiles by faith, preached the Gospel beforehand to Abraham, saying, "In you shall all the nations be blessed" (cf. Rom. 9.4-5).

A. Promise (Patriarchs)
B. Exodus and Covenant at Sinai
C. Promised Land
D. The City, the Temple, and the Throne
    (Prophet, Priest, and King)
E. Exile
F. Remnant

IV. Fullness of Time (Incarnation of the Messiah)

Gal. 4.4-5 (ESV) – But when the fullness of time had come, God sent forth his Son, born of woman, born under the law, to redeem those who were under the law, so that we might receive adoption as sons.

A. The King Comes to His Kingdom
B. The Present Reality of His Reign
C. The Secret of the Kingdom:
   the Already and the Not Yet
D. The Crucified King
E. The Risen Lord

V. The Last Times (The Descent of the Holy Spirit)

Acts 2.16-18 (ESV) – But this is what was uttered through the prophet Joel: "'And in the last days it shall be,' God declares, 'that I will pour out my Spirit on all flesh, and your sons and your daughters shall prophesy, and your young men shall see visions, and your old men shall dream dreams; even on my male servants and female servants in those days I will pour out my Spirit, and they shall prophesy.'"

A. Between the Times: the Church as
   Foretaste of the Kingdom
B. The Church as Agent of the Kingdom
C. The Conflict Between the Kingdoms of
   Darkness and Light

VI. The Fulfillment of Time (The Second Coming)

Matt. 13.40-43 (ESV) – Just as the weeds are gathered and burned with fire, so will it be at the close of the age. The Son of Man will send his angels, and they will gather out of his Kingdom all causes of sin and all lawbreakers, and throw them into the fiery furnace. In that place there will be weeping and gnashing of teeth. Then the righteous will shine like the sun in the Kingdom of their Father. He who has ears, let him hear.

A. The Return of Christ
B. Judgment
C. The Consummation of His Kingdom

VII. Beyond Time (Eternity Future)

1 Cor. 15.24-28 (ESV) – Then comes the end, when he delivers the Kingdom to God the Father after destroying every rule and every authority and power. For he must reign until he has put all his enemies under his feet. The last enemy to be destroyed is death. For "God has put all things in subjection under his feet." But when it says, "all things are put in subjection," it is plain that he is excepted who put all things in subjection under him. When all things are subjected to him, then the Son himself will also be subjected to him who put all things in subjection under him, that God may be all in all.

A. Kingdom Handed Over to God the Father
B. God as All in All

APPENDIX 10

Going Forward by Looking Back: Toward an Evangelical Retrieval of the Great Tradition

Rev. Dr. Don L. Davis

Rediscovering the "Great Tradition"

In a wonderful little book, Ola Tjorhom[1] describes the Great Tradition of the Church (sometimes called the "classical Christian tradition") as "living, organic, and dynamic."[2] The Great Tradition represents that evangelical, apostolic, and catholic core of Christian faith and practice which came largely to fruition from 100-500 AD.[3] Its rich legacy and treasures represent the Church's confession of what the Church has always believed, the worship that the ancient, undivided Church celebrated and embodied, and the mission that it embraced and undertook.

While the Great Tradition neither can substitute for the Apostolic Tradition (i.e., the authoritative source of all Christian faith, the Scriptures), nor should it overshadow the living presence of Christ in the Church through the Holy Spirit, it is still authoritative and revitalizing for the people of God. It has and still can provide

---

1   Ola Tjorhom, *Visible Church–Visible Unity: Ecumenical Ecclesiology and "The Great Tradition of the Church."* Collegeville, Minnesota: Liturgical Press, 2004. Robert Webber defined the Great Tradition in this way: "[It is] the broad outline of Christian belief and practice developed from the Scriptures between the time of Christ and the middle of the fifth century." Robert E. Webber, *The Majestic Tapestry.* Nashville: Thomas Nelson Publishers, 1986, p. 10.

2   Ibid., p. 35.

3   The core of the Great Tradition concentrates on the formulations, confessions, and practices of the Church's first five centuries of life and work. Thomas Oden, in my judgment, rightly asserts that ". . . most of what is enduringly valuable in contemporary biblical exegesis was discovered by the fifth century" (cf. Thomas C. Oden, *The Word of Life.* San Francisco: HarperSanFrancisco, 1989, p. xi.).

God's people through time with the substance of its confession and faith. The Great Tradition has been embraced and affirmed as authoritative by Catholic, Orthodox, Anglican, and Protestant theologians, those ancient and modern, as it has produced the seminal documents, doctrines, confessions, and practices of the Church (e.g., the canon of Scriptures, the doctrines of the Trinity, the deity of Christ, etc.).

Many evangelical scholars today believe that the way forward for dynamic faith and spiritual renewal will entail looking back, not with sentimental longings for the "good old days" of a pristine, problem- free early church, or a naive and even futile attempt to ape their heroic journey of faith. Rather, with a critical eye to history, a devout spirit of respect for the ancient Church, and a deep commitment to Scripture, we ought to rediscover through the Great Tradition the seeds of a new, authentic, and empowered faith. We can be transformed as we retrieve and are informed by the core beliefs and practices of the Church before the horrible divisions and fragmentations of Church history.

Well, if we do believe we ought to at least look again at the early Church and its life, or better yet, are convinced even to retrieve the Great Tradition for the sake of renewal in the Church – what exactly are we hoping to get back? Are we to uncritically accept everything the ancient Church said and did as "gospel," to be truthful simply because it is closer to the amazing events of Jesus of Nazareth in the world? Is old "hip," in and of itself?

No. We neither accept all things uncritically, nor do we believe that old, in and of itself, is truly good. Truth for us is more than ideas or ancient claims; for us, truth was incarnated in the person of Jesus of Nazareth, and the Scriptures give authoritative and final claim to the meaning of his revelation and salvation in history. We cannot accept things simply because they are reported to have been done in the past, or begun in the past. Amazingly, the Great Tradition itself argued for us to be critical, to contend for the faith once delivered to the saints (Jude 3), to embrace and celebrate the tradition received from the Apostles, rooted and interpreted by the Holy Scriptures themselves, and expressed in Christian confession and practice.

Core Dimensions of the Great Tradition

While Tjorhom offers his own list of ten elements of the theological content of the Great Tradition that he believes is worthy of reinterpretation and regard,[4] I believe there are seven dimensions that, from a biblical and spiritual vantage point, can enable us to understand what the early Church believed, how they worshiped and lived, and the ways they defended their living faith in Jesus Christ. Through their allegiance to the documents, confessions, and practices of this period, the ancient Church bore witness to God's salvation promise in the midst of a pagan and crooked generation. The core of our current faith and practice was developed in this era, and deserves a second (and twenty-second) look.

Adapting, redacting, and extending Tjorhom's notions of the Great Tradition, I list here what I take to be, as a start, a simple listing of the critical dimensions that deserve our undivided attention and wholehearted retrieval.

1. *The Apostolic Tradition.* The Great Tradition is rooted in the Apostolic Tradition, i.e., the apostles' eyewitness testimony and firsthand experience of Jesus of Nazareth, their authoritative witness to his life and work recounted in the Holy Scriptures, the canon of our Bible today. The Church is apostolic, built

---

4   Ibid., pp. 27-29. Tjorhom's ten elements are argued in the context of his work where he also argues for the structural elements and the ecumenical implications of retrieving the Great Tradition. I wholeheartedly agree with the general thrust of his argument, which, like my own belief, makes the claim that an interest in and study of the Great Tradition can renew and enrich the contemporary Church in its worship, service, and mission.

on the foundation of the prophets and the apostles, with Christ himself being the Cornerstone. The Scriptures themselves represent the source of our interpretation about the Kingdom of God, that story of God's redemptive love embodied in the promise to Abraham and the patriarchs, in the covenants and experience of Israel, and which culminates in the revelation of God in Christ Jesus, as predicted in the prophets and explicated in the apostolic testimony.

2. *The Ecumenical Councils and Creeds, Especially the Nicene Creed.* The Great Tradition declares the truth and sets the bounds of the historic orthodox faith as defined and asserted in the ecumenical creeds of the ancient and undivided Church, with special focus on the Nicene Creed. Their declarations were taken to be an accurate interpretation and commentary on the teachings of the apostles set in Scripture. While not the source of the Faith itself, the confession of the ecumenical councils and creeds represents the substance of its teachings,[5] especially those before the fifth century (where virtually all of the elemental doctrines concerning God, Christ, and salvation were articulated and embraced).[6]

---

5   I am indebted to the late Dr. Robert E. Webber for this helpful distinction between the source and the substance of Christian faith and interpretation.

6   While the seven ecumenical Councils (along with others) are affirmed by both Catholic and Orthodox communions as binding, it is the first four Councils that are to be considered the critical, most essential confessions of the ancient, undivided Church. I and others argue for this largely because the first four articulate and settle once and for all what is to be considered our orthodox faith on the doctrines of the Trinity and the Incarnation (cf. Philip Schaff, *The Creeds of Christendom*, v. 1. Grand Rapids: Baker Book House, 1996, p. 44). Similarly, even the magisterial Reformers embraced the teaching of the Great Tradition, and held its most significant confessions as authoritative. Correspondingly, Calvin could argue in his own theological interpretations that "Thus councils would come to have the majesty that is their due; yet in the meantime Scripture would stand out in the higher place, with everything subject to its standard. In this way, we willingly embrace and reverence as holy the early councils, such as those of Nicea, Constantinople, the first of

3. *The Ancient Rule of Faith.* The Great Tradition embraced the substance of this core Christian faith in a rule, i.e., an ancient standard rule of faith, that was considered to be the yardstick by which claims and propositions regarding the interpretation of the biblical faith were to be assessed. This rule, when applied reverently and rigorously, can clearly allow us to define the core Christian confession of the ancient and undivided Church expressed clearly in that instruction and adage of Vincent of Lerins: "that which has always been believed, everywhere, and by all."[7]

4. *The Christus Victor Worldview.* The Great Tradition celebrates and affirms Jesus of Nazareth as the Christ, the promised Messiah of the Hebrew Scriptures, the risen and exalted Lord, and Head of the Church. In Jesus of Nazareth alone, God has reasserted his reign over the universe, having destroyed death in his dying, conquering God's enemies through his incarnation, death, resurrection, and ascension, and ransoming humanity

---

Ephesus I, Chalcedon, and the like, which were concerned with refuting errors–in so far as they relate to the teachings of faith. For they contain nothing but the pure and genuine exposition of Scripture, which the holy Fathers applied with spiritual prudence to crush the enemies of religion who had then arisen" (cf. John Calvin, *Institutes of the Christian Religion*, IV, ix. 8. John T. McNeill, ed. Ford Lewis Battles, trans. Philadelphia: Westminster Press, 1960, pp. 1171-72).

7   This rule, which has won well-deserved favor down through the years as a sound theological yardstick for authentic Christian truth, weaves three cords of critical assessment to determine what may be counted as orthodox or not in the Church's teaching. St. Vincent of Lerins, a theological commentator who died before 450 AD, authored what has come to be called the "Vincentian canon, a three-fold test of catholicity: quod ubique, quod semper, quod ab omnibus creditum est (what has been believed everywhere, always and by all). By this three- fold test of ecumenicity, antiquity, and consent, the church may discern between true and false traditions." (cf. Thomas C. Oden, *Classical Pastoral Care*, vol. 4. Grand Rapids: Baker Books, 1987, p. 243).

from its penalty due to its transgression of the Law. Now resurrected from the dead, ascended and exalted at the right hand of God, he has sent the Holy Spirit into the world to empower the Church in its life and witness. The Church is to be considered the people of the victory of Christ. At his return, he will consummate his work as Lord. This worldview was expressed in the ancient Church's confession, preaching, worship, and witness. Today, through its liturgy and practice of the Church Year, the Church acknowledges, celebrates, embodies, and proclaims this victory of Christ: the destruction of sin and evil and the restoration of all creation.

5. *The Centrality of the Church.* The Great Tradition confidently confessed the Church as the people of God. The faithful assembly of believers, under the authority of the Shepherd Christ Jesus, is now the locus and agent of the Kingdom of God on earth. In its worship, fellowship, teaching, service, and witness, Christ continues to live and move. The Great Tradition insists that the Church, under the authority of its undershepherds and the entirety of the priesthood of believers, is visibly the dwelling of God in the Spirit in the world today. With Christ himself being the Chief Cornerstone, the Church is the temple of God, the body of Christ, and the temple of the Holy Spirit. All believers, living, dead, and yet unborn – make up the one, holy, catholic (universal), and apostolic community. Gathering together regularly in believing assembly, members of the Church meet locally to worship God through Word and sacrament, and to bear witness in its good works and proclamation of the Gospel. Incorporating new believers into the Church through baptism, the Church embodies the life of the Kingdom in its fellowship, and demonstrates in word and deed the reality of the Kingdom of God through its life together and service to the world.

6. *The Unity of the Faith.* The Great Tradition affirms unequivocally the catholicity of the Church of Jesus Christ, in that it is concerned with keeping communion and continuity with the worship and theology of the Church throughout the ages (Church universal). Since there has been and can only be one hope, calling, and faith, the Great Tradition fought and strove for oneness in word, in doctrine, in worship, in charity.

7. *The Evangelical Mandate of the Risen Christ.* The Great Tradition affirms the apostolic mandate to make known to the nations the victory of God in Jesus Christ, proclaiming salvation by grace through faith in his name, and inviting all peoples to repentance and faith to enter into the Kingdom of God. Through acts of justice and righteousness, the Church displays the life of the Kingdom in the world today, and through its preaching and life together provides a witness and sign of the Kingdom present in and for the world (*sacramentum mundi*), and as the pillar and ground of the truth. As evidence of the Kingdom of God and custodians of the Word of God, the Church is charged to define clearly and defend the faith once for all delivered to the Church by the apostles.

Conclusion: Finding Our Future by Looking Back

In a time where so many are confused by the noisy chaos of so many claiming to speak for God, it is high time for us to rediscover the roots of our faith, to go back to the beginning of Christian confession and practice, and see, if in fact, we can recover our identity in the stream of Christ worship and discipleship that changed the world. In my judgment, this can be done through a critical, evangelical appropriation of the Great Tradition, that core belief and practice which is the source of all our traditions, whether Catholic, Orthodox, Anglican, or Protestant.

Of course, specific traditions will continue to seek to express and live out their commitment to the Authoritative Tradition (i.e., the Scriptures) and Great Tradition through their worship, teaching, and service. Our diverse Christian traditions (little "t"), when they are rooted in and expressive of the teaching of Scripture and led by the Holy Spirit, will continue to make the Gospel clear within new cultures or sub-cultures, speaking and modeling the hope of Christ into new situations shaped by their own set of questions posed in light of their own unique circumstances. Our traditions are essentially movements of contextualization, that is they are attempts to make plain within people groups the Authoritative Tradition in a way that faithfully and effectively leads them to faith in Jesus Christ.

We ought, therefore, to find ways to enrich our contemporary traditions by reconnecting and integrating our contemporary confessions and practices with the Great Tradition. Let us never forget that Christianity, at its core, is a faithful witness to God's saving acts in history. As such, we will always be a people who seek to find our futures by looking back through time at those moments of revelation and action where the Rule of God was made plain through the incarnation, passion, resurrection, ascension, and soon-coming of Christ. Let us then remember, celebrate, reenact, learn afresh, and passionately proclaim what believers have confessed since the morning of the empty tomb – the saving story of God's promise in Jesus of Nazareth to redeem and save a people for his own.

How to PLANT a Church
Rev. Dr. Don L. Davis

> Mark 16.15-18 (ESV) – And he said to them, "Go into all
> the world and proclaim the gospel to the whole creation.
> [16] Whoever believes and is baptized will be saved, but
> whoever does not believe will be condemned. [17] And these
> signs will accompany those who believe: in my name they
> will cast out demons; they will speak in new tongues; [18] they
> will pick up serpents with their hands; and if they drink any
> deadly poison, it will not hurt them; they will lay their hands
> on the sick, and they will recover."

I. Prepare

> Luke 24.46-49 (ESV) – and he said to them, "Thus it is written,
> that the Christ should suffer and on the third day rise from
> the dead, and that repentance and forgiveness of sins should
> be proclaimed in his name to all nations, beginning from
> Jerusalem. You are witnesses of these things. And behold,
> I am sending the promise of my Father upon you. But stay
> in the city until you are clothed with power from on high."

A. Form a church-plant team.

B. Pray.

C. Select a target area and population.

D. Do demographic and ethnographic studies.

II. Launch

> Gal. 2.7-10 (ESV) – On the contrary, when they saw that I had
> been entrusted with the gospel to the uncircumcised, just as

Peter had been entrusted with the gospel to the circumcised
(for he who worked through Peter for his apostolic ministry
to the circumcised worked also through me for mine to the
Gentiles), and when James and Cephas and John, who seemed
to be pillars, perceived the grace that was given to me, they
gave the right hand of fellowship to Barnabas and me, that
we should go to the Gentiles and they to the circumcised. Only,
they asked us to remember the poor, the very thing I was
eager to do.

A. Recruit and train volunteers.

B. Conduct evangelistic events and door-to-door evangelism.

EQUIP

Eph. 4.11-16 (ESV) – And he gave the apostles, the prophets,
the evangelists, the pastors and teachers, [12] to equip the
saints for the work of ministry, for building up the body of
Christ, [13] until we all attain to the unity of the faith and of
the knowledge of the Son of God, to mature manhood, to
the measure of the stature of the fullness of Christ, [14] so
that we may no longer be children, tossed to and fro by the
waves and carried about by every wind of doctrine, by human
cunning, by craftiness in deceitful schemes. [15] Rather,
speaking the truth in love, we are to grow up in every way
into him who is the head, into Christ, [16] from whom the
whole body, joined and held together by every joint with
which it is equipped, when each part is working properly,
makes the body grow so that it builds itself up in love.

III. Assemble

Acts 2.41-47 (ESV) – So those who received his word were
baptized, and there were added that day about three thousand
souls. And they devoted themselves to the apostles' teaching

and fellowship, to the breaking of bread and the prayers. And awe came upon every soul, and many wonders and signs were being done through the apostles. And all who believed were together and had all things in common. And they were selling their possessions and belongings and distributing the proceeds to all, as any had need. And day by day, attending the temple together and breaking bread in their homes, they received their food with glad and generous hearts, praising God and having favor with all the people. And the Lord added to their number day by day those who were being saved.

A. Form cell groups, Bible studies, etc. to follow up new believers, to continue evangelism, and to identify and train emerging leaders.

B. Announce the birth of a new church to the neighborhood and meet regularly for public worship, instruction and fellowship.

IV. Nurture

1 Thess. 2.5-9 (ESV) – For we never came with words of flattery, as you know, nor with a pretext for greed – God is witness. Nor did we seek glory from people, whether from you or from others, though we could have made demands as apostles of Christ. But we were gentle among you, like a nursing mother taking care of her own children. So, being affectionately desirous of you, we were ready to share with you not only the gospel of God but also our own selves, because you had become very dear to us. For you remember, brothers, our labor and toil: we worked night and day, that we might not be a burden to any of you, while we proclaimed to you the gospel of God.

A. Develop individual and group discipleship.

B. Fill key roles in the church: identify and use spiritual gifts.

EMPOWER

Acts 20.28 (ESV) – Pay careful attention to yourselves and to all the flock, in which the Holy Spirit has made you overseers, to care for the church of God, which he obtained with his own blood.

Acts 20.32(ESV) – And now I commend you to God and to the word of his grace, which is able to build you up and to give you the inheritance among all those who are sanctified.

V. Transition

Titus 1.4-5 (ESV) – To Titus, my true child in a common faith: Grace and peace from God the Father and Christ Jesus our Savior. This is why I left you in Crete, so that you might put what remained into order, and appoint elders in every town as I directed you –

A. Transfer leadership to indigenous leaders so they become self-governing, self-supporting and self-reproducing (appoint elders and pastors).

B. Finalize decisions about denominational or other affiliations.

C. Commission the church.

D. Foster association with World Impact and other urban churches for fellowship, support, and mission ministry.

How to PLANT a Church

EVANGELIZE

PREPARE

- Form a church-plant team.
- Pray.
- Select a target area and population.
- Do demographic and ethnographic studies.

LAUNCH

- Recruit and train volunteers.
- Conduct evangelistic events and door-to-door evangelism.

EQUIP

ASSEMBLE

- Form cell groups, Bible studies, etc. to follow up new believers, to continue evangelism, and to identify and train emerging leaders.
- Announce the birth of a new church to the neighborhood and meet regularly for public worship, instruction and fellowship.

NURTURE

- Develop individual and group discipleship.
- Fill key roles in the church; identify and use spiritual gifts.

EMPOWER

TRANSITION

- Transfer leadership to indigenous leaders so they become self-governing, self-supporting and self-reproducing (appoint elders and pastors).
- Finalize decisions about denominational or other affiliations.
- Commission the church.
- Foster association with World Impact and other urban churches for fellowship, support and mission ministry.

Pauline Precedents from Acts: The Pauline Cycle[1]

1. Missionaries Commissioned: Acts 13.1-4; 15.39-40; Gal. 1.15-16.

2. Audience Contacted: Acts 13.14-16; 14.1; 16.13-15; 17.16-19.

3. Gospel Communicated: Acts 13.17-41; 16.31; Rom. 10.9-14; 2 Tim. 2.8.

4. Hearers Converted: Acts. 13.48; 16.14-15; 20.21; 26.20; 1 Thess. 1.9-10.

5. Believers Congregated: Acts 13.43; 19.9; Rom 16.4-5; 1 Cor. 14.26.

6. Faith Confirmed: Acts 14.21-22; 15.41; Rom 16.17; Col. 1.28; 2 Thess. 2.15; 1 Tim. 1.3.

7. Leadership Consecrated; Acts 14.23; 2 Tim. 2.2; Titus 1.5.

8. Believers Commended; Acts 14.23; 16.40; 21.32 (2 Tim. 4.9 and Titus 3.12 by implication).

9. Relationships Continued: Acts 15.36; 18.23; 1 Cor. 16.5; Eph. 6.21-22; Col. 4.7-8.

10. Sending Churches Convened: Acts 14.26-27; 15.1-4.

---

1   The "Pauline Cycle" terminology, stages, and diagram are taken from David J. Hesselgrave, *Planting Churches Cross- Culturally*, 2nd ed. Grand Rapids: Baker Book House, 2000.

"Evangelize, Equip, and Empower" and "P.L.A.N.T." schemas for church planting taken from *Crowns of Beauty: Planting Urban Churches Conference Binder* Los Angeles: World Impact Press, 1999.

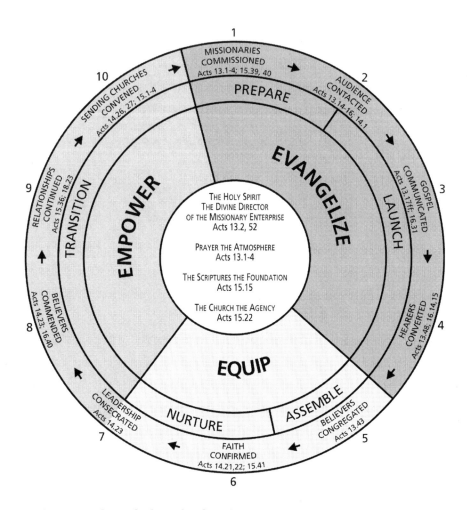

Ten Principles of Church Planting

1. *Jesus is Lord.* (Matt. 9.37-38) All church plant activity is made effective and fruitful under the watch care and power of the Lord Jesus, who himself is the Lord of the harvest.

2. *Evangelize, Equip, and Empower unreached people to reach people.* (1 Thess. 1.6-8) Our goal in reaching others for Christ is not only for solid conversion but also for dynamic multiplication; those who are reached must be trained to reach others as well.

3. *Be inclusive: whosoever will may come.* (Rom. 10.12) No strategy should forbid any person or group from entering into the Kingdom through Jesus Christ by faith.

4. *Be culturally neutral: Come just as you are.* (Col. 3.11) The Gospel places no demands on any seeker to change their culture as a prerequisite for coming to Jesus; they may come just as they are.

5. *Avoid a fortress mentality.* (Acts 1.8) The goal of missions is not to create an impregnable castle in the midst of an unsaved community, but a dynamic outpost of the Kingdom which launches a witness for Jesus within and unto the very borders of their world.

6. *Continue to evangelize to avoid stagnation.* (Rom. 1.16-17) Keep looking to the horizons with the vision of the Great Commission in mind; foster an environment of aggressive witness for Christ.

7. *Cross racial, class, gender, and language barriers.* (1 Cor. 9.19-22) Use your freedom in Christ to find new, credible ways to communicate the kingdom message to those farthest from the cultural spectrum of the traditional church.

8. *Respect the dominance of the receiving culture.* (Acts 15.23-29) Allow the Holy Spirit to incarnate the vision and the ethics of the Kingdom of God in the words, language, customs, styles, and experience of those who have embraced Jesus as their Lord.

9. *Avoid dependence.* (Eph. 4.11-16) Neither patronize nor be overly stingy towards the growing congregation; do not underestimate the power of the Spirit in the midst of even the smallest Christian community to accomplish God's work in their community.

10. *Think reproducibility.* (2 Tim. 2.2; Phil. 1.18) In every
    activity and project you initiate, think in terms of equipping
    others to do the same by maintaining an open mind
    regarding the means and ends of your missionary endeavors.

Resources for Further Study

Cornett, Terry G. and James D. Parker. "Developing Urban
    Congregations: A Framework for World Impact Church
    Planters." *World Impact Ministry Resources.* Los Angeles:
    World Impact Press, 1991.

Davis, Don L. and Terry G. Cornett. "An Outline for a Theology
    of the Church." *Crowns of Beauty: Planting Urban Churches*
    (Training Manual). Los Angeles: World Impact Press, 1999.

Hesselgrave, David J. *Planting Churches Cross Culturally:
    A Biblical Guide.* Grand Rapids: Baker Book House, 2000.

Hodges, Melvin L. *The Indigenous Church: A Handbook on How
    to Grow Young Churches.* Springfield, MO: Gospel Publishing
    House, 1976.

Shenk, David W. and Ervin R. Stutzman. *Creating Communities
    of the Kingdom: New Testament Models of Church Planting.*
    Scottsdale, PA: Herald Press, 1988.

In Christ

Rev. Dr. Don L. Davis

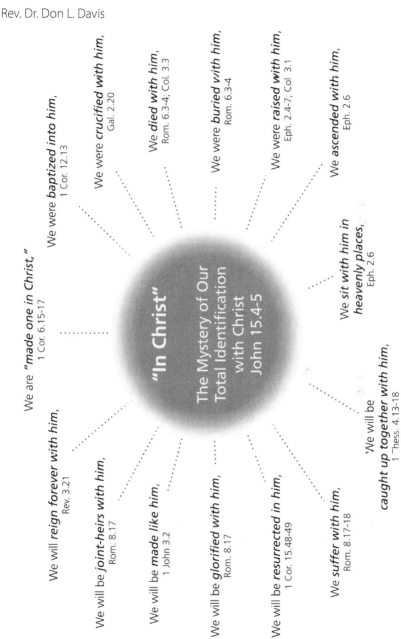

"In Christ"

The Mystery of Our Total Identification with Christ
John 15.4-5

We are "*made one in Christ*," 1 Cor. 6.15-17

We were *baptized into him*, 1 Cor. 12.13

We were *crucified with him*, Gal. 2.20

We *died with him*, Rom. 6.3-4; Col. 3.3

We were *buried with him*, Rom. 6.3-4

We were *raised with him*, Eph. 2.4-7; Col 3.1

We *ascended with him*, Eph. 2.6

We *sit with him in heavenly places*, Eph. 2.6

We will be *caught up together with him*, 1 Thess. 4.13-18

We *suffer with him*, Rom. 8.17-18

We will be *resurrected in him*, 1 Cor. 15.48-49

We will be *glorified with him*, Rom. 8.17

We will be *made like him*, 1 John 3.2

We will be *joint-heirs with him*, Rom. 8.17

We will *reign forever with him*, Rev. 3.21

APPENDIX 13

Jesus of Nazareth: The Presence of the Future

Rev. Dr. Don L. Davis

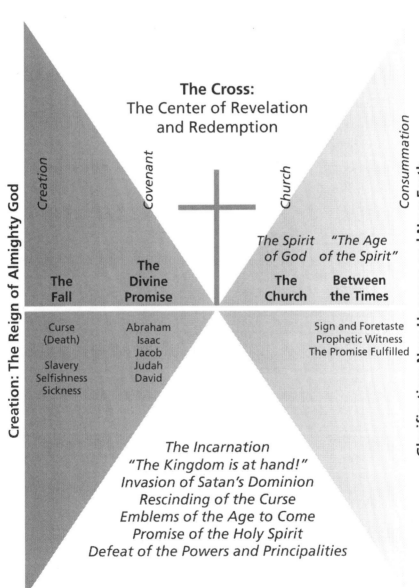

Appendix 14

Living in the Already and the Not Yet Kingdom

Rev. Dr. Don L. Davis

The Spirit: The pledge of the inheritance (*arrahon*)
The Church: The foretaste (*aparche*) of the Kingdom
"In Christ": The rich life (*en Christos*) we share as citizens of the Kingdom

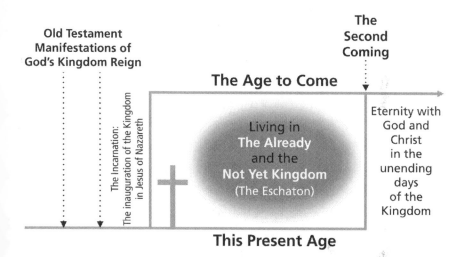

Internal enemy: The flesh (*sarx*) and the sin nature
External enemy: The world (*kosmos*) the systems of greed, lust, and pride
Infernal enemy: The devil (*kakos*) the animating spirit of falsehood and fear

Jewish View of Time

The Coming of Messiah
The restoration of Israel
The end of Gentile oppression
The return of the earth to Edenic glory
Universal knowledge of the Lord

APPENDIX 15

Let God Arise! The Seven "A's" of Seeking the Lord . . .

Rev. Dr. Don L. Davis

		THEME	
"Seek the Lord" Zechariah 8.18-23 · Isaiah 55.6	1	Adoration	• Delight and Enjoyment in God • Overwhelming Gratefulness • Acknowledging God in his Person and Works
	2	Admission	• Powerlessness • Helplessness • Awareness of One's Desperate Need for God
	3	Availability	• Dying to preoccupation with self and love of the world • No confidence in fleshly wisdom, resources, or method • Consecrating ourselves as living sacrifices to God
"Entreat the Favor of the Lord" Zechariah 8.18-23 · Jeremiah 33.3	4	Awakening *Global and Local*	• Refreshment: outpouring of the Holy Spirit on God's people • Renewal: Obedience to the Great Commandment - Loving God and neighbor • Revolution: Radical new orientation to Christ as Lord
	5	Advancement *Global and Local*	• Movements: outreaches to unreached, pioneer regions • Mobilization: of every assembly to fulfill the Great Commission • Military mindset: Adopting a warfare mentality to suffer and endure hardness in spiritual warfare
	6	Affirmation	• Giving Testimony over what the Lord has done • Challenging one another by speaking the truth in Love
	7	Acknowledgment	• Waiting patiently on God to act by his timing and methods • Living confidently as though God is answering our petitions • Acting as if God will do precisely what he says he will do

. . . and Entreating His Favor

SCRIPTURE	AWARENESS		CONCERT OF PRAYER
Ps. 29.1 2 Rev. 4-11 Rom. 11.33-36 Ps. 27.4-8	Of God's Majestic Glory	God's Face	Gather to Worship and Pray
Ps. 34.18-19 Prov. 28.13 Dan. 4.34-35 Isa. 30.1-5	Of Our Brokenness before God		Confess Your Powerlessness
Rom. 12.1-5 John 12.24 Phil. 3.3-8 Gal. 6.14	Of Our Yieldedness to God		Surrender Your All to Christ
Hos. 6.1-3 Eph. 3.15-21 Matt. 22.37-40 John 14.15	Asking for the Spirit's Filling	Fullness	Fervently Intercede on Behalf of Others
Acts 1.8 Mark 16.15-16 Matt. 28.18-20 Matt. 11.12 Luke 19.41-42 2 Tim. 2.1-4	Asking for the Spirit's Moving	Fulfillment	
Ps. 107.1-2 Heb. 3.13 2 Cor. 4.13 Mal. 3.16-18	The Redeemed Saying So	The Faith	Encourage One Another in Truth and Testimony
Ps. 27.14 2 Chron. 20.12 Prov. 3.5-6 Isa. 55.8-11 Ps. 2.8	Keeping Our Eyes on the Lord	The Fight	Scatter to Work and Wait

APPENDIX 16

The Nicene Creed with Biblical Support

The Urban Ministry Institute

We believe in one God, *(Deut. 6.4-5; Mark 12.29; 1 Cor. 8.6)*
    the Father Almighty, *(Gen. 17.1; Dan. 4.35; Matt. 6.9; Eph. 4.6; Rev. 1.8)*
    Maker of heaven and earth *(Gen. 1.1; Isa. 40.28; Rev. 10.6)*
    and of all things visible and invisible. *(Ps. 148; Rom. 11.36; Rev. 4.11)*

We believe in one Lord Jesus Christ, the only Begotten Son of
    God, begotten of the Father before all ages, God from God,
    Light from Light, True God from True God, begotten not
    created, of the same essence as the Father, *(John 1.1-2; 3.18; 8.58;*
        14.9-10; 20.28; Col. 1.15, 17; Heb. 1.3-6)
    through whom all things were made. *(John 1.3; Col. 1.16)*

Who for us men and for our salvation came down from heaven and
    was incarnate by the Holy Spirit and the Virgin Mary and became
    human. *(Matt. 1.20-23; John 1.14; 6.38; Luke 19.10)*
    Who for us too, was crucified under Pontius Pilate, suffered and
    was buried. *(Matt. 27.1-2; Mark 15.24-39, 43-47; Acts 13.29; Rom. 5.8;*
        Heb. 2.10; 13.12)
    The third day he rose again according to the Scriptures,
        (Mark 16.5-7; Luke 24.6-8; Acts 1.3; Rom. 6.9; 10.9; 2 Tim. 2.8)
    ascended into heaven, and is seated at the right hand of the
    Father. *(Mark 16.19; Eph. 1.19-20)*
    He will come again in glory to judge the living and the
    dead, and his Kingdom will have no end. *(Isa. 9.7; Matt. 24.30;*
        John 5.22; Acts 1.11; 17.31; Rom. 14.9; 2 Cor. 5.10; 2 Tim. 4.1)

We believe in the Holy Spirit, the Lord and life-giver, *(Gen. 1.1-2;*
Job 33.4; Ps. 104.30; 139.7-8; Luke 4.18-19; John 3.5-6; Acts 1.1-2;
1 Cor. 2.11; Rev. 3.22)
who proceeds from the Father and the Son, *(John 14.16-18, 26;*
15.26; 20.22)
who together with the Father and Son is worshiped and glorified,
(Isa. 6.3; Matt. 28.19; 2 Cor. 13.14; Rev. 4.8)
who spoke by the prophets.
(Num. 11.29; Mic. 3.8; Acts 2.17-18; 2 Pet. 1.21)
We believe in one holy, catholic, and apostolic Church.
(Matt. 16.18; Eph. 5.25-28; 1 Cor. 1.2; 10.17; 1 Tim. 3.15; Rev. 7.9)

We acknowledge one baptism for the forgiveness of sin,
(Acts 22.16; 1 Pet. 3.21; Eph. 4.4-5)
And we look for the resurrection of the dead
And the life of the age to come. *(Isa. 11.6-10; Mic. 4.1-7; Luke 18.29-30;*
Rev. 21.1-5; 21.22-22.5)
Amen.

Memory Verses

Below are suggested memory verses, one for each section of
the Creed.

The Father

Rev. 4.11 (ESV) – Worthy are you, our Lord and God, to receive
glory and honor and power, for you created all things, and by
your will they existed and were created.

The Son

John 1.1 (ESV) – In the beginning was the Word, and the Word
was with God, and the Word was God.

The Son's Mission

1 Cor. 15.3-5 (ESV) – For what I received I passed on to you as of first importance: that Christ died for our sins according to the Scriptures, that he was buried, that he was raised on the third day according to the Scriptures, and that he appeared to Peter, and then to the Twelve.

The Holy Spirit

Rom. 8.11 (ESV) – If the Spirit of him who raised Jesus from the dead dwells in you, he who raised Christ Jesus from the dead will also give life to your mortal bodies through his Spirit who dwells in you.

The Church

1 Pet. 2.9 (ESV) – But you are a chosen race, a royal priesthood, a holy nation, a people for his own possession, that you may proclaim the excellencies of him who called you out of darkness into his marvelous light.

Our Hope

1 Thess. 4.16-17 (ESV) – For the Lord himself will descend from heaven with a cry of command, with the voice of an archangel, and with the sound of the trumpet of God. And the dead in Christ will rise first. Then we who are alive, who are left, will be caught up together with them in the clouds to meet the Lord in the air, and so we will always be with the Lord.

Appendix 17

Once Upon a Time: The Cosmic Drama through a Biblical Narration of the World
Rev. Dr. Don L. Davis

From Everlasting to Everlasting, Our Lord Is God

From everlasting, in that matchless mystery of existence before time began, our Triune God dwelt in perfect splendor in eternal community as Father, Son, and Holy Spirit, the I AM, displaying his perfect attributes in eternal relationship, needing nothing, in boundless holiness, joy, and beauty. According to his sovereign will, our God purposed out of love to create a universe where his splendor would be revealed, and a world where his glory would be displayed and where a people made in his own image would dwell, sharing in fellowship with him and enjoying union with himself in relationship, all for his glory.

Who, as the Sovereign God, Created a World That Would Ultimately Rebel against His Rule

Inflamed by lust, greed, and pride, the first human pair rebelled against his will, deceived by the great prince, Satan, whose diabolical plot to supplant God as ruler of all resulted in countless angelic beings resisting God's divine will in the heavenlies. Through Adam and Eve's disobedience, they exposed themselves and their heirs to misery and death, and through their rebellion ushered creation into chaos, suffering, and evil. Through sin and rebellion, the union between God and creation was lost, and now all things are subject to the effects of this great fall – alienation, separation, and condemnation become the underlying reality for all things. No angel, human being, or creature can solve this dilemma, and without God's direct intervention, all the universe, the world, and all its creatures would be lost.

Yet, in Mercy and Loving-kindness, the Lord God Promised to Send a Savior to Redeem His Creation

In sovereign covenantal love, God determined to remedy the effects of the universe's rebellion by sending a Champion, his only Son, who would take on the form of the fallen pair, embrace and overthrow their separation from God, and suffer in the place of all humankind for its sin and disobedience. So, through his covenant faithfulness, God became directly involved in human history for the sake of their salvation. The Lord God stoops to engage his creation for the sake of restoring it, to put down evil once and for all, and to establish a people out of which his Champion would come to establish his reign in this world once more.

So, He Raised Up a People from Which the Governor Would Come

And so, through Noah, he saves the world from its own evil, through Abraham, he selects the clan through which the seed would come. Through Isaac, he continues the promise to Abraham, and through Jacob (Israel) he establishes his nation, identifying the tribe out of which he will come (Judah). Through Moses, he delivers his own from oppression and gives them his covenantal law, and through Joshua, he brings his people into the land of promise. Through judges and leaders he superintends his people, and through David, he covenants to bring a King from his clan who will reign forever. Despite his promise, though, his people fall short of his covenant time after time. Their stubborn and persistent rejection of the Lord finally leads to the nation's judgment, invasion, overthrow, and captivity. Mercifully, he remembers his covenant and allows a remnant to return – for the promise and the story were not done.

Who, as Champion, Came Down from Heaven, in the Fullness of Time, and Won through the Cross

Some four hundred years of silence occurred. Yet, in the fullness of time, God fulfilled his covenant promise by entering into this realm of evil, suffering, and alienation through the incarnation. In the person of Jesus of Nazareth, God came down from heaven and lived among us, displaying the Father's glory, fulfilling the requirements of God's moral law, and demonstrating the power of the Kingdom of God in his words, works, and exorcisms. On the Cross he took on our rebellion, destroyed death, overcame the devil, and rose on the third day to restore creation from the Fall, to make an end of sin, disease, and war, and to grant never-ending life to all people who embrace his salvation.

And, Soon and Very Soon, He Will Return to This World and Make All Things New

Ascended to the Father's right hand, the Lord Jesus Christ has sent the Holy Spirit into the world, forming a new people made up of both Jew and Gentile, the Church. Commissioned under his headship, they testify in word and deed the gospel of reconciliation to the whole creation, and when they have completed their task, he will return in glory and complete his work for creation and all creatures. Soon, he will put down sin, evil, death, and the effects of the Curse forever, and restore all creation under its true rule, refreshing all things in a new heavens and new earth, where all beings and all creation will enjoy the shalom of the Triune God forever, to his glory and honor alone.

And the Redeemed Shall Live Happily Ever After . . .

The End

Appendix 18

Overview of Church Plant Planning Phases

Rev. Dr. Don L. Davis

	Prepare	Launch	
Definition	Forming a team of called members who ready themselves to plant a church under the Holy Spirit's direction	Penetrating the selected community by conducting evangelistic events among the target population	→
Purpose	Seek God regarding the target population and community, the formation of your church plant team, organizing strategic intercession for the community, and doing research on its needs and opportunities	Mobilize team and recruit volunteers to conduct ongoing evangelistic events and holistic outreach to win associates and neighbors to Christ	→
Parent-Child Metaphor	Decision and Conception	Pre-natal Care	→
Question Focus During Dialogue	Questions about: • Preparing your team • The target community • Strategic prayer initiatives • Demographic studies	Questions about: • Character and number of evangelistic events • Communication and advertisement of events • Recruiting and coordinating volunteers • Identity and name of the outreach	→
Cardinal Virtue	Openness to the Lord	Courage to engage the community	→
Cardinal Vices	Presumption and "paralysis of analysis"	Intimidation and haughtiness	→
Bottom Line	Cultivate a period of listening and reflecting	Initiate your engagement with boldness and confidence	→

Assemble	Nurture	Transition
Gathering the cells of converts together to form a local assembly of believers, announcing the new church to the neighbors in the community	Nurturing member and leadership discipleship, enabling members to function in their spiritual gifts, and establishing solid infrastructure within the Christian assembly	Empowering the church for independence by equipping leaders for autonomy, transferring authority, and creating structures for financial independence
Form cell groups, Bible studies, or home fellowships for follow-up, continued evangelism, and ongoing growth toward public birth of the church	Develop individual and group discipleship by filling key roles in the body based on burden and gifting of members	Commission members and elders, install pastor, and foster church associations
Childbirth	Growth and Parenting	Maturity to Adulthood
Questions about: • Follow-up and incorporation of new believers • Make-up of small group life • The character of public worship • Initial church structures and procedures • Initial body life and growth • Cultural friendliness of church	Questions about: • Discipling individuals and leaders • Helping members identify gifts and burdens (teams) • Credentials for leadership • Church order, government and discipline	Questions about: • Incorporation • Affiliations and associations • Transferring leadership • Missionary transition • Ongoing reproduction
Wisdom to discern God's timing	Focus upon the faithful core	Dependence on the Spirit's ability
Impatience and cowardice	Neglect and micromanagement	Paternalism and quick release
Celebrate the announcement of your body with joy	Concentrate on investing in the faithful	Pass the baton with confidence in the Spirit's continued working

APPENDIX 19

A Schematic for a Theology
of the Kingdom and the Church

Rev. Dr. Don L. Davis

The Father	The Son
Love - 1 John 4.8 Maker of heaven and earth and of all things visible and invisible.	Faith - Heb. 12.2 Prophet, Priest, and King

→

Creation	Kingdom
The triune God, Yahweh Almighty, is the Creator of all things, the Maker of the universe.	The Reign of God expressed in the rule of his son Jesus the Messiah.

→

The eternal God, Yahweh Almighty, is the triune Lord of all, Father, Son, and Holy Spirit, who is sovereign in power, infinite in wisdom, perfect in holiness, and steadfast in love. All things are from him, and through him and to him as the source and goal of all things.

O, the depth of the riches and wisdom and knowledge of God! How unsearchable are his judgments, and how inscrutable his ways! For who has known the mind of the Lord, or who has been his counselor? Or who has ever given a gift to him, that he might be repaid?" For from him and through him and to him are all things. To him be glory forever! Amen! - Rom. 11.33-36 (ESV) (cf. 1 Cor. 15.23-28; Rev. 21.1-5)

Freedom
(Through the fall, the Slavery of Satan and sin now controls creation and all the creatures of the world. Christ has brought freedom and release through his matchless work on the Cross and the Resurrection, Rom. 8.18-21!)

Jesus answered them, "Truly, truly, I say to you, everyone who commits sin is a slave to sin. The slave does not remain in the house forever; the son remains forever. So if the Son sets you free, you will be free indeed." - John 8.34-36 (ESV)

Wholeness
(Through the Fall, Sickness [dis-ease] has come into the world. Christ has become our healing and immortality through the Gospel, Rev. 21.1-5!)

But he was wounded for our transgressions; he was crushed for our iniquities; upon him was the chastisement that brought us peace, and with his stripes we are healed. - Isa. 53.5 (ESV)

Justice
(Through the Fall, Selfishness now dominates the relationships of the world. Christ has brought his own justice and righteousness to the Kingdom, Isa. 11.6-9!)

Behold, my servant whom I have chosen, my beloved with whom my soul is well pleased. I will put my Spirit upon him, and he will proclaim justice to the Gentiles. He will not quarrel or cry aloud, nor will anyone hear his voice in the streets; a bruised reed he will not break, and a smoldering wick he will not quench, until he brings justice to victory. - Matt. 12.18-20 (ESV)

→

→

→

The Spirit
Hope - Rom. 15.13
Lord of the Church

Church
The Holy Spirit now indwells the one, holy, catholic, and apostolic community of Christ, which functions as a witness to (Acts 28.31) and a foretaste of (Col. 1.12; James 1.18; 1 Pet. 2.9; Rev. 1.6) the everlasting Kingdom of God.

*The Church Is a Catholic (universal), Apostolic Community Where the Word Is **Rightly Preached**. Therefore It Is a Community of:*

Calling - For freedom Christ has set us free; stand firm therefore, and do not submit again to a yoke of slavery. - Gal. 5.1 (ESV) (cf. Rom. 8.28-30; 1 Cor. 1.26-31; Eph. 1.18; 2 Thess. 2.13-14; Jude 1.1)

Faith - ". . . for unless you believe that I am he you will die in your sins". . . . So Jesus said to the Jews who had believed in him, "If you abide in my word, you are truly my disciples, and you will know the truth, and the truth will set you free." - John 8.24b, 31-32 (ESV) (cf. Ps. 119.45; Rom. 1.17; 5.1-2; Eph. 2.8-9; 2 Tim. 1.13-14; Heb. 2.14-15; James 1.25)

Witness - The Spirit of the Lord is upon me, because he has anointed me to proclaim good news to the poor. He has sent me to proclaim liberty to the captives and recovering of sight to the blind, to set at liberty those who are oppressed, to proclaim the year of the Lord's favor. - Luke 4.18-19 (ESV) (cf. Lev. 25.10; Prov. 31.8; Matt. 4.17; 28.18-20; Mark 13.10; Acts 1.8; 8.4, 12; 13.1-3; 25.20; 28.30-31)

*The Church Is One Community Where the Sacraments Are **Rightly Administered**. Therefore It Is a Community of:*

Worship - You shall serve the Lord your God, and he will bless your bread and your water, and I will take sickness away from among you. - Exod. 23.25 (ESV) (cf. Ps. 147.1-3; Heb. 12.28; Col. 3.16; Rev. 15.3-4; 19.5)

Covenant - And the Holy Spirit also bears witness to us; for after the saying, "This is the covenant that I will make with them after those days, declares the Lord: I will put my laws on their hearts, and write them on their minds," then he adds, "I will remember their sins and their lawless deeds no more." - Heb. 10.15-17 (ESV) (cf. Isa. 54.10-17; Ezek. 34.25-31; 37.26-27; Mal. 2.4-5; Luke 22.20; 2 Cor. 3.6; Col. 3.15; Heb. 8.7-13; 12.22-24; 13.20-21)

Presence - In him you also are being built together into a dwelling place for God by his Spirit. - Eph. 2.22 (ESV) (cf. Exod. 40.34-38; Ezek. 48.35; Matt. 18.18-20)

*The Church Is a Holy Community Where Discipline Is **Rightly Ordered**. Therefore It Is a Community of:*

Reconciliation - For he himself is our peace, who has made us both one and has broken down in his flesh the dividing wall of hostility by abolishing the law of commandments and ordinances, that he might create in himself one new man in place of the two, so making peace, and might reconcile us both to God in one body through the cross, thereby killing the hostility. And he came and preached peace to you who were far off and peace to those who were near. For through him we both have access in one Spirit to the Father. - Eph. 2.14-18 (ESV) (cf. Exod. 23.4-9; Lev. 19.34; Deut. 10.18-19; Ezek. 22.29; Mic. 6.8; 2 Cor. 5.16-21)

Suffering - Since therefore Christ suffered in the flesh, arm yourselves with the same way of thinking, for whoever has suffered in the flesh has ceased from sin, so as to live for the rest of the time in the flesh no longer for human passions but for the will of God. - 1 Pet. 4.1-2 (ESV) (cf. Luke 6.22; 10.3; Rom. 8.17; 2 Tim. 2.3; 3.12; 1 Pet. 2.20-24; Heb. 5.8; 13.11-14)

Service - But Jesus called them to him and said, "You know that the rulers of the Gentiles lord it over them, and their great ones exercise authority over them. It shall not be so among you. But whoever would be great among you must be your servant, and whoever would be first among you must be your slave even as the Son of Man came not to be served but to serve, and to give his life as a ransom for many." - Matt. 20.25-28 (ESV) (cf. 1 John 4.16-18; Gal. 2.10)

Spiritual Growth Diagram 1

Leroy Eims, *The Lost Art of Discipling*. Grand Rapids: Zondervan, 1978. p. 124.

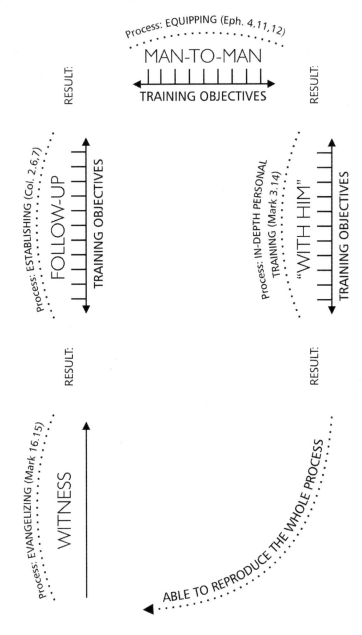

Spiritual Growth Diagram 2

Adapted from Rick Warren, *The Purpose-Driven Church*. p. 144.

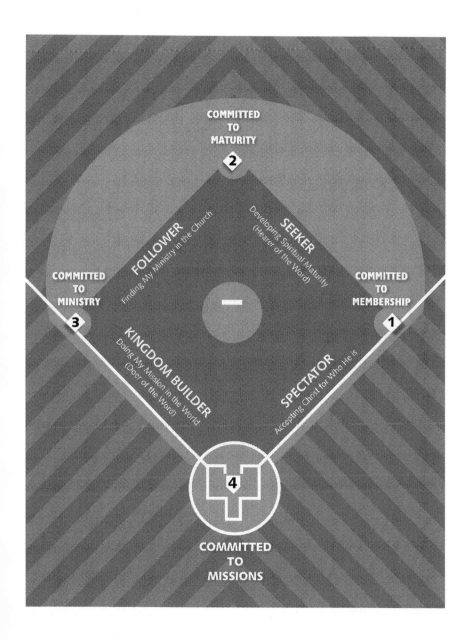

APPENDIX 22

Steps to Equipping Others

Rev. Dr. Don L. Davis

Step One

You become a Master at it, striving toward mastery by practicing it with regularity, excellence, and enjoyment. You must learn to do it, and do it excellently. While you need not be perfect, you should be able to do it, be doing it regularly, and growing in your practice of it. This is the most fundamental principle of all mentoring and discipling. You cannot teach what you do not know or cannot do, and when your Apprentice is fully trained, they will become like you (Luke 6.40).

Step Two

You select an Apprentice who also desires to develop mastery of the thing, one who is teachable, faithful, and available. Jesus called the Twelve to be with him, and to send them out to preach (Mark 3.14). His relationship was clear, neither vague nor coerced. The roles and responsibilities of the relationship must be carefully outlined, clearly discussed, and openly agreed upon.

Step Three

You instruct and model the task in the presence of and accompanied by your Apprentice. He/she comes alongside you to listen, observe, and watch. You do it with regularity and excellence, and your Apprentice comes along "for the ride," who is brought along to see how it is done. A picture is worth a thousand words. This sort of non-pressure participant observation is critical to in-depth training (2 Tim. 2.2; Phil. 4.9).

Step Four

You do the task and practice the thing together. Having modeled the act for your Apprentice in many ways and at many times, you now invite them to cooperate with you by becoming a partner-in-training, working together on the task. The goal is to do the task together, taking mutual responsibility. You coordinate your efforts, working together in harmony to accomplish the thing.

Step Five

Your Apprentice does the task on their own, in the presence of and accompanied by you. You provide opportunity to your Apprentice to practice the thing in your presence while you watch and listen. You make yourself available to help, but offer it in the background; you provide counsel, input, and guidance as they request it, but they do the task. Afterwards, you evaluate and clarify anything you may have observed as you accompanied your Apprentice (2 Cor. 11.1).

Step Six

Your Apprentice does the thing solo, practicing it regularly, automatically, and excellently until mastery of the thing is gained. After your Apprentice has done the task under your supervision excellently, he/she is ready to be released to make the thing his/her own by habituating the act in his/her own life. You are a co-doer with your Apprentice; both of you are doing the task without coercion or aid from the other. The goal is familiarity and skillfulness in the task (Heb. 5.11-15).

Step Seven

Your Apprentice becomes a Mentor of others, selecting other faithful Apprentices to equip and train. The training process bears fruit when the Apprentice, having mastered the thing you have equipped him/her to do, becomes a trainer of others. This is the heart of the discipling and training process (Heb. 5.11-14; 2 Tim. 2.2).

APPENDIX 23

The Way of Wisdom

Rev. Dr. Don L. Davis

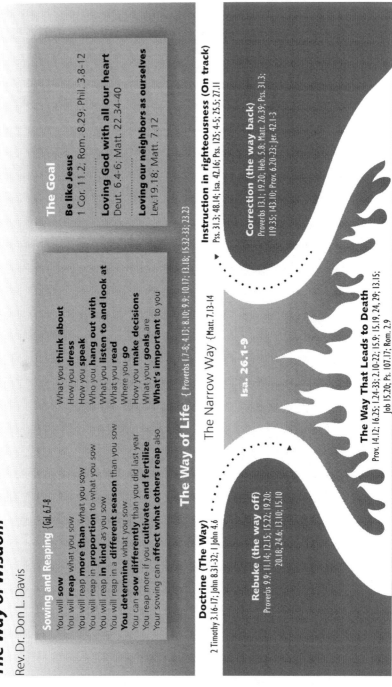

Sowing and Reaping {Gal. 6.7-8}

You will **sow**
You will **reap** what you sow
You will reap **more than** what you sow
You will reap in **proportion** to what you sow
You will reap **in kind** as you sow
You will reap in a **different season** than you sow
You determine what you sow
You can **sow differently** than you did last year
You reap more if you **cultivate and fertilize**
Your sowing can **affect what others reap** also

What you **think about**
How you **dress**
How you **speak**
Who you **hang out with**
What you **listen to and look at**
What you **read**
Where you **go**
How you **make decisions**
What your **goals** are
What's important to you

The Goal

Be like Jesus
1 Cor. 11.2; Rom. 8.29; Phil. 3.8-12

Loving God with all our heart
Deut. 6.4-6; Matt. 22.34-40

Loving our neighbors as ourselves
Lev. 19.18; Matt. 7.12

The Way of Life { Proverbs 1.7-8; 4.13; 8.10; 9.9; 10.17; 13.18; 15.32-33; 23.23

Instruction in righteousness (On track)
Pss. 31.3; 48.14; Isa. 42.16; Pss. 125; 4-5; 25.5; 27.11

The Narrow Way {Matt. 7.13-14

Correction (the way back)
Proverbs 13.1; 19.20; Heb. 5.8; Matt. 26.39; Pss. 31.3; 119.35; 143.10; Prov. 6.20-23; Jer. 42.1-3

Isa. 26.1-9

The Way That Leads to Death
Prov. 14.12; 16.25; 1.24-33; 2.10-22; 15.9; 15.19, 24, 29; 13.15; Job 15.20; Ps. 107.17; Rom. 2.9

Doctrine (The Way)
2 Timothy 3.16-17; John 8.31-32; 1 John 4.6

Rebuke (the way off)
Proverbs 9.9; 11.14; 12.15; 15.22; 19.20; 20.18; 24.6; 13.10; 15.10

Made in the USA
Middletown, DE
01 February 2025

70690247R00144